CW00433659

KNOWING YOUR ENEMY

David W Measures

D W M M I PUBLISHING

ISBN 0-9549564-0-0

All scripture texts are taken from the New King James version of the Bible unless stated otherwise.

British Library Cataloguing in Publication Data.
A catalogue record for this book is available from the British Library.

Published by
D W M M I Publishing
www.knowingyourenemy.com

Layout of Author's electronic files
and production by
MOORLEYS
Print & Publishing, Ilkeston

CONTENTS

FOREWORD

This, I believe, is the first in a series of Holy Spirit inspired books by David Measures. **Knowing your Enemy** is a book that will teach and inspire Christians on a number of key issues. It will remove the scales from eyes and minds and open up new ways of using the Word in believer's lives daily.

David and Helen Measures have been the principal keystone in my walk towards and with Jesus Christ. David's discernment and ministry, concerning deliverance from the effects of the enemy, has been an astonishing blessing to me in learning about the Word and the Power we have through Jesus Christ to lead a Holy Spirit filled life. I have witnessed, through David's ministry, some fantastic changes in believer's lives when released from the grip of the enemy.

I am convinced that this book you are about to read will inspire you and highlight to you the many revelations that will bring about significant positive changes in your walk with Jesus Christ. It is an honour and a joy for me to recommend this book to you and I know that within it you will find the freedom you may require.

IAN GRAY

Acknowledgments

I wish to give a special thanks to Helen my wife, and partner in the ministry in using the wisdom the Lord has given her also for her help in producing this book.

I would like to thank Ian Gray and Elaine Kirk for their help with the proof reading of the book. Also I would like to thank Scott Gamble for his tireless work in helping to put it all on to paper. I would like to thank the people who have kindly allowed me to publish their testimonies of the Lord's grace and goodness to them. I am sure that these true accounts will be a help and a blessing for many people who are going through similar experiences.

Introduction

It is only through the work of the Holy Spirit in my life that the contents of this book have come into being. The Lord has graciously used me to set many people free from the works of the enemy. Since the Lord set this captive free in 1989. For over twenty-five years I was tormented by a demon, which caused me to have a sleep problem that was rooted in fear, after watching a horror film at the age of thirteen years. The film involved hypnosis and it affected me to the point that I actually felt the demon enter me like a snake, wriggling down from the top of my head to my feet and I felt evil at that point. The Lord has graciously shown me that we have a constant enemy, and has put a deep desire in my heart to follow Him. I can now appreciate the desperation and torment of others seeking an answer especially in the Body of Christ.

The first time I gave a testimony and ministered, spirits manifested themselves and were expelled. Sometimes this shocked the congregation, but it was the work of the Holy Spirit working through me. Following my dramatic conversion, and spending time at Bible School, I began to realize the Lord had called me for a special purpose.

This study is to help to expose some of the works of Satan in peoples' lives with scriptural explanations of the Lord's ministry. Some wrongly think that because Jesus defeated Satan at the Crucifixion the enemy cannot influence their life, if the latter was so then all Christians would be in perfect health for the prophet Isaiah wrote in Ch 53 v 5 "*And by His stripes we are healed.*" As we know not all Christians are instantly healed physically or emotionally upon salvation. <u>That is why one of the Holy Spirit's gifts, is the gift of Healing</u>. In the same commission that Jesus gave to his disciples He also told them to drive out demons. By accepting His commission in theory only many children of God are missing out on the blessing. Included are a few examples of the Lord's work today in people's lives where demons have been active but later expelled. I praise God that He is faithful and His Word is true, He will never let us down even though others do and we do ourselves. I do hope the contents of this book can be both enlightening and helpful to those who are seeking help. When everything seems impossible, God is still sovereign.

My prayer is that the Lord will bless you richly, as you read this book.

Pastor David W Measures

1. WE ARE AT WAR

When I was young, every week my mother took me to the graveyards to put flowers on the graves of lost loved ones. My job was to go and get the fresh water in a galvanized canister. I liked to do that because it stopped me focusing on the surroundings. Yet I noticed that virtually every age of a person could be found on the headstones, so I came to understand at an early age that death was no respecter of age or class. No one explained to me what this thing called death was all about, except that my mother had told me that they had been poorly and had gone to be with Jesus and now they were happy. I was confused because things went through my young mind like, 'it does not feel happy being in the graveyard', and 'if they are happy why can't we all be dead?' 'Why do people have to be ill?' Also my mother told me that God loves everyone. She told me that God loves me and I must try always to love Him. So I wanted to love God with all my heart, yet I thought how can I if people have to go through illness? Why, if God loves us, do we have to die? So now I was more confused. I would often go somewhere alone and cry because of my confusion. I began to even hate the idea of sickness and infirmity. Little did I know that God hated the same and He was preparing me for His service?

For there is a battle for the souls of mankind. Mankind is God's special creation made in His image and likeness with freedom to choose.

God also created a multitude of angels, and three prominent angels are named in the Bible. These are Gabriel, the messenger angel; Michael, the archangel and Lucifer, the covering angel; God created them all with free will. One of these prominent angels rebelled taking one third of the angels with him. His name was Lucifer who became Satan or the Devil after his rebellion. He is opposed to everything of God, so there is a battle for the soul of every man and woman.

When nations go to war no one knows the outcome. What will happen? Who will win? Who will lose? What will be the consequences of this war? What effect will it have upon the people who are caught up in it? Will it start all over again? How long will it last? Will I die? Will my family die? Will my life change forever? In these situations we are faced with uncertainty and fear in many areas of our lives.

Romans Ch 8 v 37 – 39 says,

> *"Yet in all these things we are more than conquerors through Him who loved us. For I am persuaded that neither death nor life, nor angels, nor principalities nor powers, nor things present nor things to come, nor height nor depth, nor any other created thing, shall be able to separate us from the love of God which is in Christ Jesus our Lord".*

In Christ we have already won. However, so many Born Again Christians (those who have personally put their trust in Jesus Christ and His finished work of the cross) are still fighting for victory, often because the enemy has placed some landmines in their lives and he has the detonator which he can activate, usually at the most inopportune moment.

Ephesians Ch 6 v 12 states,

> *"For we do not wrestle against flesh and blood, but against principalities, against powers, against the rulers of the darkness of this age, against spiritual hosts of wickedness in heavenly places".*

It is not flesh and blood which are our enemies but all the works of Satan. It is always sad when we hear of Christians slandering other Christians personally. Sometimes it seems to get like the political scene, with character assassination and social climbing. Jesus never did this. We can see here in this passage from Ephesians, it says *"heavenly places".* It is stated in Ephesians Ch 2 v 2 that Satan is named as *"the prince of the power of the air."* The Bible implies, in 2 Corinthians Ch 12 v 2, that there are three heavens as the apostle Paul said, *"he knew a man who was caught up to the third heaven into Paradise."* We do know Satan was thrown out of the presence of God, because of his rebellion, but as a spiritual being he still has access to the lower heavens and the earth where we live.

It seems as though in some cases Satan has the ability to mess us about, like one would a string puppet. If this is so we must ask ourselves what attachment has Satan to us? After all, a string puppet has to have an attachment from the person operating it. In John Ch 14 v 30 Jesus said that He could go to the Cross, as the ruler of this world (Satan) had got no hold on Him. Can we truly say that or do we just hope so. Yet the Church has far too much sickness, infirmity, emotional and mental illnesses for us to say that he has nothing in us.

The Bible is the manual for the lives of God's children, those whom He has redeemed. Many people feel that the Bible contradicts itself. I personally do not believe that is right. Our Lord is not double minded. The Bible is only for believers, as it cannot be truly understood without knowing the author. Let me explain why I say this.

1 Corinthians Ch 7 v 32 & 34 states:

But I want you to be without care. He who is unmarried cares for the things of the Lord - how he may please the Lord.

There is a difference between a wife and a virgin. The unmarried woman cares about the things of the Lord, that she may be holy both in body and in spirit.

These verses alone tell us that scripture is for believers. There are many unmarried people in the world who I am sure do not accept or apply this teaching.

The Bible tells us the Lord wishes us to be happy and joyful, healthy and whole. He has provided everything for our provision and for our enjoyment and fulfilment. That is why there is nothing more fulfilling and enriching than loving and serving Him, in whatever role He has chosen us to do.

The Bible tells us:

God gave his ONLY begotten son, the Lord Jesus Christ, Jesus is the Word of God. The Word became manifest as a man, that being the fact God has only One Word.

So why are there so many interpretations and ideas of what the scriptures are saying to mankind? As God has only One Word, surely if the scriptures say it – we should believe it, and not try to justify ourselves in disbelief on account of our circumstances, backgrounds or experiences. The Devil and his demons are just as real and active today as they have ever been and even more as the End of Time approaches. Often if you mention the Church or Christians being spiritual, so many people shy away and think they have joined a cult or a spiritualist movement or some other abominable practice. I have been asked at a church coffee morning, if I was a spiritualist because I said our fellowship often prays for the sick and healings take place. The Lord, I believe, desires the Church to be more spiritual than all the Devils' agents i.e. spiritualists, witch doctors, occult healers, new age therapists etc.

We as the Church of Jesus Christ can be victorious because we should have the beautiful Holy Spirit sent from heaven above living within us. This is what happened to the early disciples on that day of Pentecost, when the Holy Spirit came upon the believers, just as Jesus had promised. Before Jesus ascended into Heaven, He told the disciples that they would receive Power when the Holy Spirit would come upon them. On the day of Pentecost they all spoke in tongues (Acts Ch 2 v 4). It was not tongues that gave the Power, but the Power of the Holy Spirit that caused them to speak in tongues. Before this, the disciples had received the Holy Spirit through Jesus breathing upon them after His resurrection.

John Ch 20 v 22 states:

> *And when He had said this, He breathed on them, and said to them, "Receive the Holy Spirit".*

So the experience at Pentecost was extra to the receiving of the Holy Spirit the disciples received after Jesus appeared to them.

When I spoke about the Church being spiritual, of course that is God's plan.

Genesis Ch 1 v 26 God said,

> *"Let Us make man in Our image according to Our likeness".*

God is Spirit without a body. God, I believe, also has a soul (mind, emotions and will).

(1) He has a mind - all through the Bible we see how He planned for our salvation working it out for Jesus to be born just at the right time.

(2) He has emotions - the scriptures say that God can be angry; He can be grieved. The Bible tells us He is a jealous God, He is kind and He is love.

(3) He also has a will - the scriptures tell us that it is not His will that any should perish but that all should come to repentance.

Man is Spirit and Soul with a Body. The Body dies and is usually either buried or cremated – the Spirit goes back to God. The scriptures say and our Soul (our mind, emotions and will) lives forever. Jesus explained this in Luke Ch 16 v 19-28.

> "*There was a certain rich man who was clothed in purple and fine linen and fared sumptuously every day. But there was a certain beggar named Lazarus, full of sores, who was laid at the gate, desiring to be fed with the crumbs which fell from the rich man's table. Moreover the dogs came and licked his sores. So it was that the beggar died, and was carried by the angels to Abraham's bosom. The rich man also died and was buried. And being in torments in Hades, he lifted up his eyes and saw Abraham afar off and Lazarus in his bosom*".

We see here the rich man, even though he was dead, his soul was very much alive. The scripture states that he was in torment, proving he had feelings, and he also lifted up his eyes, proving he had a will.

> *"Then he cried and said, Father Abraham, have mercy on me, and send Lazarus that he may dip the tip of his finger in water and cool my tongue; for I am tormented in this flame."*

Proving he had a mind, he made up his mind that he did not like where he was and he wanted mercy. Again we see he had feelings because his tongue was burning.

But Abraham said,

> *"Son remember that in your lifetime you received your good things, and likewise Lazarus evil things; but now he is comforted and you are tormented. And besides all this, between us and you there is a great gulf fixed, so that those who want to pass from here to you cannot, nor can those from there pass to us." Then he said, "I beg you therefore, father that you would send him to my father's house, for I have five brothers that he may testify to them, lest they also come to this place of torment."*

The rich man, even though he had no love for Lazarus when he was alive, still had emotions towards his own family even when dead. His selfishness carried on into eternity.

This story shows us that all of mankind will live forever. It will either be in Heaven or it will be in Hell. We will know things, be able to feel things and will have a will.

Some people say this is only a parable, yet Jesus never said it was a parable, but even if it is, the same applies. A parable is a story based on a spiritual truth.

Jesus warned His disciples in Matthew Ch 24 that in the last days there will be wars and rumours of wars. Not only was He warning about physical wars but I believe spiritual ones as well. This is described in the book of Revelation Ch 13. The battle in the last days will get much stronger as the Devil realizes that his time is short.

Even with all the Devil's schemes, the Lord has given His Church the ability to stand against him, with His Word to guide us through all difficulties. We need to be like David when he wrote Psalm 27.

The Lord is my light and my salvation;
Whom shall I fear?
The Lord is my strength of my life;
Of whom shall I be afraid?
When the wicked came against me
To eat up my flesh,
They stumbled and fell.

Though an army should encamp against me,
My heart shall not fear,
Though war should rise against me,
In this I will be confident.

The new birth of the Holy Spirit is essential for us to even see the Kingdom of Heaven. There has to be a change of direction in our lives. No-one is born a Christian; a person has to become one. There has to be a time in our lives, when we alone have to come before God with our life. The first words John the Baptist spoke to the Jews in Matthew Ch 3 v 2 were:

"Repent for the Kingdom of Heaven is at hand."

The Jews certainly knew what He was talking about; it was not as though this man was just being an eccentric and shouting anything that came into his head. The reader must understand that every Sabbath the Jews had been remembering the exodus from Egypt, when they had the Passover meal. Moses had led the children of Israel out from Egypt, out of the hands of Pharaoh, with God working through him doing great signs and miracles. Joshua was called to take over the leadership after the death of Moses and it was Joshua who was chosen for the job of leading the Children of Israel into the Promised Land.

Joshua Ch. 3 v 5 states:

And Joshua said to the people, "Sanctify yourselves, for tomorrow the Lord will do wonders among you."

All the twelve tribes of Israel did just that. The priests were ordered to take with them the Ark of the Covenant which housed the Ten Commandments that the Lord had given to Moses, and stand in the midst of the Jordan River. As soon as they did so, the river stopped flowing and the people walked over on dry ground.

Joshua Ch 4 v 1-9 states:

And it came to pass, when all the people had completely crossed over the Jordan that the Lord spoke to Joshua, saying: "Take for yourselves twelve men from the people, one man from every tribe, and command them saying, Take for yourselves twelve stones from here, out of the midst of the Jordan, from the place where the priests' feet stood firm. You shall carry them over with you and leave them in the lodging place where you lodge tonight." Then Joshua called the twelve men whom he had appointed from the children of Israel' one man from every tribe; and Joshua said to them: "Cross over before the ark of the Lord your God into the midst of the Jordan, and each one of you take up a stone on his shoulder, according to the number of tribes of the children of Israel, that this may be a sign among you when your children ask in time to come, saying 'what do these stones mean to you?' Then you shall answer them that the waters of the Jordan were cut off before the Ark of the Covenant of the Lord; when it crossed the Jordan, the waters of the Jordan were cut off. And these stones shall be for a memorial to the children of Israel forever." And the children of Israel did so, just as Joshua had commanded, and took up twelve stones from the midst of the Jordan, as the Lord had spoken to Joshua, according to the number of the tribes of the children of Israel, and carried them over to the place where they lodged, and laid them down there. Then Joshua set up twelve stones in the midst of the Jordan, in the place where the feet of the priests who bore the Ark of the Covenant stood; and they are there to this day.

The people sanctified themselves; one man from each of the tribes took a stone out of the Jordan which represented unity of all the tribes. These men carried the stones on their shoulders. They took the burden of the unity agreement. They took the stones to their lodging place until the time when the stones were set up in a place called Gilgal, sometime later. Joshua replaced the stones taken out of the Jordan with twelve more, signifying the Lord's acceptance of their dedication to Him. The priests stood in the Jordan River with their feet firmly placed on firm ground.

When John the Baptist was standing in the river preaching repentance very likely he would have either been in the exact spot, or if not, he certainly would have been referring to the time of the covenant with God and the children of Israel before they were allowed into the Promised Land. Since that time the people had strayed far away from the Lord.

The first message Jesus preached in Matthew Ch 4 v17 was

"Repent for the Kingdom of heaven is at hand"

The same message of repentance was Peter's first message, Paul's first message and the twelve disciples' first message. What is the present day church's first message?

If the foundation is not firmly established the building will eventually start to crack until it falls or it has to be taken down as it is unsafe. From my experience of twenty-five years as a builder, I certainly know that this is true. I may have patched, and made costly repairs, but it would never be one hundred percent. Without a proper foundation the building would still have to be taken down and start afresh and all the cost, time and effort would have been a waste.

John Ch 3 v 3 states:

> ***Jesus answered and said to him, "Most assuredly, I say to you unless one is born again, he cannot see the Kingdom of God".***

If you then couple this scripture with John Ch 1 v 12–13 which states:

> *"But as many as received Him, to them He gave the right to become children of God, to those who believe in his name; who were born, not of blood, nor of the will of the flesh, nor of the will of man, but of God".*

We see that to be 'Born again' is a totally different experience to our natural birth. Being 'Born of God,' we need to be able to grasp what the Lord is saying. The words 'Born again' are used so much in Christian circles that I believe that the truth can be misunderstood. Now in some translations of the Bible, they use the words 'Born anew' which I prefer (which means again but in a different form).

Proverbs Ch 23 v 7,

"For as he thinks in his heart so is he."

If I only believe I have been given another chance I may make the same mistakes I did before, and if so it could leave me feeling condemned. Now if I believe that I've been 'Born from above' things are different. I pray that you the reader will understand this Divine Truth. The fact is that if you have been 'Born from above' you have been purchased with a very high price – the precious Blood of Christ. Jesus gave His all so we as believers could be saved, healed and delivered. The Bible tells us that by His stripes we have been healed. The price for healing and deliverance has already been paid for.

Many Spirit filled Churches today, do not believe that a Christian can be influenced by a satanic influence (demon). They may say that a Christian can only be oppressed (from without) as though the demons can only be on the outside looking in. Many do not believe that a demon can live inside a Christian. There are others however, who do accept this, but are unwilling to move in the ministry of deliverance. Now I know that not all ministries are the same, but the church needs to be open to the Lord in all the facets of His ministry. Otherwise Satan will deceive them and take them captive. I have included in the book instances where Jesus cast out demons and in every case they were from believers. The fact is Jesus gave us a commission, and as far as I can see, this has never been rescinded. This is a Divine call for the Church – Mark Ch 16 v 15-18.

Preach the Word
Heal the sick
Cast out demons.

How can we truly expect to be blessed by God if we purposely neglect the call of God? He has commissioned His servants to do these three tasks and has equipped His children to undertake such wonderful work. We may have to ask ourselves – are we building our church or the Kingdom of God. Jesus said He will build His Church and the gates of Hell shall not prevail against it. Surely we have a wonderful example of the Christian ministry when we look to our Commander in Chief.

2. JESUS
OUR COMMANDER IN CHIEF

When we make the decision to follow in our Lord's footsteps, we should have the same desire as He does to Save, Heal and Deliver. All through the Gospels we see Him tirelessly at work, guided by the Holy Spirit. He turned no one away who came to Him; He supplied their needs, even provided food for over five thousand people. In compassion He did something in every situation. I believe He's expecting no less from His disciples today. It's a tough challenge but nevertheless it is the truth. He has equipped the Church with all the tools for the job and given the talents and gifts to go with them. If Jesus cast out the demons two thousand years ago why should we think that for the last two thousand years there has not been any to cast out? In my experience this is vital for the Kingdom of God to bring the Kingdom onto the Earth. If you have never opened your heart up to the Gospel in this way, maybe this little book will be of help to you. Jesus said:

"It is enough for the disciple to be like his teacher".
(Matthew Ch 10 v 25).

When we see our Commander in Chief in action we just read in amazement. After receiving salvation, for a time I felt quite sad that I had been born in the twentieth century. Two thousand years ago, fishing in a boat would have been my choice, being called to follow Him. Yet it took me quite some time in my new life in Jesus to realise that He wanted me to be His disciple today. He has called you if you are a believer to be His disciple, to do the work He did and to do even greater miracles.

One day Jesus entered the synagogue.
Mark Ch 1 v 21.

Then they went into Capernaum, and immediately on the Sabbath He entered the synagogue and taught. And they were astonished at his teaching, for he taught as one having authority, not as the scribes. Now there was a man in the synagogue with an unclean spirit. And he cried out saying, "Let us alone! What have we to do with you, Jesus of Nazareth? Did you come to destroy us? I know who you are - The Holy One of God!" But Jesus rebuked him, saying "Be quiet, and come out of him!" And when the unclean spirit had convulsed him and cried out in a loud voice, he came out of him. Then they were all amazed, so that they questioned among themselves saying, "What is this? What new doctrine is this? For with authority He commands even the unclean spirits, and they obey Him". And immediately his fame spread throughout the region around Galilee.

This man was in the synagogue and yet the man had an unclean spirit (singular). The man came to Jesus; the unclean spirit spoke and said 'Let us alone' (plural). Jesus cast the unclean spirit (singular) out of the man. This is interesting. You have heard the saying 'Birds of a feather flock together. If you look in the sky at migration time you do not see all different birds flying together, it is always the same flock. Well, spirits do recognize each other. This spirit in the man recognized he had friends and that is why he said 'us'. Rebellious people will be happy in each other's company. People who are happy with the certain beliefs and doctrines of that church or denomination will flock together. If a person does not wish to be convicted or challenged they will search for a church fellowship that suits their needs. If you want Jesus and His word to be central in your own life then you will only be happy in a fellowship that wants the same. I believe the Lord had no double mindedness in Him when the Holy Spirit inspired the Prophets and the Apostles to write the scriptures. So if we are the body of Christ and Christ is not a schizophrenic,

why are there so many different doctrines in His Body?

Could it be that spirits are very much alive in the Church today? Could this be why there is so much church hopping in our generation? The scriptures call them wandering stars (Christians wandering from church to church). Wrong spirits can be affecting the Church because of the reluctance to accept the Word of God as it is. It was the same in the Apostle John's day.

1 John Ch 2 v 18-19.

Little children, it is the last hour; and as you have heard that the Antichrist is coming, even now many antichrists have come, by which we know that it is the last hour. They went out from us, but they were not of us; for if they had been of us, they would have continued with us; but they went out that they might be made manifest, that none of them were of us.

These people, who the Apostle John is talking about, were once part of the Church they were obviously listening to the teachings of the Apostles, in accordance with the Holy Scriptures, because the word states that they went out from among them. Why did they leave? The Apostle John called them 'antichrist spirits'. I too on occasions have challenged people to blot out the passage of the Bible that in their opinion is not the Word of God. If everyone who did not believe some part did that, the Bible might just be left with the maps.

As we read the scriptures in Acts Ch 5 v 12 we notice that as the Apostles met each day in the temple courts by Solomon's Porch, mighty miracles were done by them but no one dared to join them. Nevertheless God added to their number those who were being saved. One day when Jesus was speaking to the multitudes, His disciples were present at the same time. His mother and brothers came to take Him away. His answer was: Matthew Ch 12 v 48-50.

"Who is My mother and who are My brothers?" And He stretched out His Hand towards His disciples and said, "Here are My Mother and My brothers! "For whoever does the will of my Father in heaven is my brother and sister and mother."

It seemed that Jesus only recognized those who were doing the Father's Will. As Christians we need to really seek the Father to do His Will.

The scriptures tell us that Jesus spent many hours in prayer before He went about doing His miracles. Each morning He would go onto a hillside or remote place to commune with God the

Father. It took Him hours in prayer to know the Father's will yet only seconds to perform a miracle.

Jesus went into the villages teaching and healing those in need. People brought their sick and demon possessed and He healed them all. How do we know that God will not use us all to heal the sick if we do not allow Him to? We might be pleasantly surprised to find that as we make a decision to move in faith, God has already gone before us and will continually be with us. The Bible says in the Gospel of Mark Ch 1 v 37 that "everyone was seeking Him", actually that is the same today. People are looking for answers for all of life's problems – looking for the meaning of life and trying to find the answer in religions or ungodly theories like evolution. It is surprising that so many Christian ministers sadly believe in evolution because prominent scientists say they can prove it. The Bible does not say; "In the beginning science created God." God created everything before scientists existed. It is true everyone is seeking Him but they do no realise it. They are seeking everything that Christ can give them but unfortunately the answer is too easy for them. People are seeking happiness, waiting for something to happen to make them happy. Even if they have the good fortune for it to happen it is only short lived for it often leaves them needing more.

Being part of God's family we can have joy that will never leave us whether times are good or bad. Multitudes are seeking for healing of their bodies and their souls (mind, emotions and their will) all the places where the Devil has been allowed to get a foothold into their lives, either by their own actions or by the evil influences of other people. So they try to get help from the occult or many of the occult practices that are in the market place today. Practices like reflexology, homeopathy, crystal therapy, aroma-therapy, acupuncture, reiki healing etc, all of them based in the New Age religion. Sadly these can be found advertised in monthly church magazines. The Word of God tells us to rely on Him; not to get involved in ungodly practices. Even though the therapists do show Christian symbols in their shops or even worse have an influence in the church congregation. Necromancy, Spiritualism, Fortune Telling, in whatever form, is described in the Bible as an abomination to God. Even if it was seventy years ago when the people were involved, they will very likely need deliverance from the influence. In ministry I have found this to be true. People have even relived the original experience when something similar happened later in their life. In one particular case the time span was seventy-six years. So many times people will tell me, when asked if they have been involved in occult practices, that they only visited a fortune teller as a bit of fun and that was when they were young and it was also before they were a Christian. Some have asked for forgiveness but never sought for deliverance from the spiritual power behind the sin. True and pure healing can only be found in the Lord Jesus Christ.

The Master gave Himself and all that He had, for however many who came to Him, He never promoted Himself. I believe neither should we? The Bible tells us that God will lift us up. We need to be very careful as Christians not to use Christianity as a business and put fellow Christians under undue pressure, all to promote ourselves.

If we read John Ch 7 v 1 – 8

> *After these things Jesus walked in Galilee: for he would not walk in Judea, because the Jews sought to kill Him. Now the Jews' Feast of Tabernacles was at hand His brothers therefore said to Him. "Depart from here and go into Judea that your disciples also may see the works that you are doing. For no one does any thing in secret while he himself seeks to be known openly. If you do these things, show yourself to the world." For neither did his brethren believe in Him. Then Jesus said unto them, "My time is not yet come, but your time is always ready. The world cannot hate you; but it hates me because I testify of it that its works are evil .You go up to this feast. I am not yet going up to this feast, for My time is not yet fully come".*

His brothers thought He should promote Himself, make a name for Himself, and go to the Feast. He was not interested in going to the Feast with His brothers. Eventually He went on His own accord. Jesus never compromised with the world's ideas. Our Commander in Chief is a shining example of what we should be. Are all our motives the same as our Lord's, or are we building the house out of the wrong materials? The First Epistle to the Corinthians explains in detail.

1 Corinthians Ch3 v 9-15.

For we are God's fellow workers; you are God's field, you are God's building. According to the grace of God which was given to me, as a wise master builder I have laid the foundation, and another builds on it. But let each one take heed how he builds on it. For no other foundation can anyone lay than which is laid, which is Jesus Christ. Now if anyone builds on this foundation with gold, silver, precious stones, wood, hay, straw, each one's work will become clear; for the Day will declare it, because it will be revealed by fire and the fire will test each one's work, of what sort it is. If anyone's work which he has built on it endures, he will receive a reward If anyone's work is burned, he will suffer loss; but he himself will be saved, yet so as through fire.

We need, with the help of the Holy Spirit to analyse ourselves to find out what makes us do what we do. As we read these verses we need to examine our motives with good works that seem right to us (gold, silver, precious stones) but even these so called precious things will be burned up if the Lord has not planned it. We have been called to be His servants not to do our own thing. If we truly look at our motives some of us might fall short of God's ways. So why is this? I believe it is because; either we refuse to accept His ideals (rebellion), or we do not let Him change us, we want to do it our way, (stubbornness)

1 Samuel Ch 15 v 23 states:

For rebellion is as the sin of witchcraft and stubbornness is as iniquity and idolatry.

If the problem is not one of these then maybe the enemy has his hold on us from outside influences. The Bible tells us not to give him a foothold. If we give him an inch he will take a mile!

1 Thessalonians Ch 5 v 23 states:

Now may the God of peace Himself sanctify you completely; and may your whole Spirit, Soul, and Body be preserved blameless at the coming of our Lord Jesus Christ.

The Body: The Bible tells us we should be given as a living sacrifice to God. The Soul is our real person, God says

Our Mind should be renewed by the word of God. He also says

Our Emotions should be the same as that of Christ and

Our Will should line up with God's will.

Our Spirit belongs to God (Note: it is the spirit that is Born Again [Anew]). However, most of our problems lie in the soul and that is where the demons want to live. They affect our emotions, they try to control our minds and they try to make us do their will or our own will, but not Gods' will. This is what happened in the Garden of Eden when the serpent tricked the woman. Adam and his wife were perfect at that time, yet they became deceived. Since that time he has been tricking and deceiving all mankind. He even had the gall to try and trick our Commander in Chief but he found his match with Jesus. Jesus beat him on every occasion. We will now look at our Commander In Chief in action throughout the accounts in the gospels, and see the miracles that the people received.

3. FIGHTING FIT

The Church along with most of the world have access to all the medical services, including hospitals, doctors and a wide range of 'healing' drugs. But the Church has, or should have, Jesus the Master Healer reigning. He healed everyone He touched, and if the Bible is true and Jesus is the same yesterday, today and forever, then we should expect the same today. I personally believe the

Church of God should be the healthiest place on the face of the earth.

Sickness and infirmity was not God's original idea, God said to Adam in Genesis Ch 2 v 17:

> *"But the tree of the knowledge of good and evil you shall not eat, for in the day that you eat of it you shall surely die".*

As there had not been any death at that time, I guess Adam would not have known what death was. But he might have known what separation from God was, as the scriptures tell us that God came to Adam and his wife in the cool of the day. It seemed very likely the Lord left him alone for the rest of the time. Sin separates us from the presence of God today, and if not repented of, it will separate us for eternity.

The Lord has provided the answer for our dilemma in and through His Word. All too often people do not understand His Word or why it was written. What is worse, they may have been willing to put their trust in the Lord for healing, only to find the church they attend does not accept healing? Many churches believe all God's spritual gifts became obsolete after the time of the original Apostles.

Satan the Devil is behind all our sicknesses and diseases. If God promoted sickness and death, why did Jesus heal all and raise people from the dead? So many people calling themselves Christians do not believe in Divine Healing, or they cannot accept that it could be for them. This is sad, because the Lord has paid for it at Calvary. Some may think that there are more worthy cases than themselves and feel the Lord is limited in His healing power as though His healings and miracles are on ration. Could it be that this thinking is based on guilt, unbelief or false humility (pride). Some think that it is God's trial for them, or even God gave them sickness or infirmity so they can feel suffering. I do not believe so. After all, how can it be when we read scriptures like Proverbs Ch 4 v 20 – 22?

> *My son, give attention to my words, incline your ear to my sayings. Do not let them depart from your eyes; keep them in the midst of your heart; for they are life to those who find them, and health to all your flesh.*

The Lord is still healing today as He was two thousand years ago, we will look at the story of the infirm woman in Luke Ch 13 v 10 - 16.

> *Now He was teaching in one of the synagogues on the Sabbath. And behold, there was a woman who had a spirit of infirmity eighteen years, and was bent over and could in no way raise herself up. But when Jesus saw her, He called her to Him and said to her "Woman, you are loosed from your infirmity." And He laid His hands on her, and immediately she was made straight, and glorified God. But the ruler of the synagogue answered with indignation, because Jesus had healed on the Sabbath; and he said to the crowd, "There are six days on which men ought to work; therefore come and be healed on them, and not on the Sabbath day." The Lord then answered him and said, "Hypocrite! Does not each one of you on the Sabbath loose his Ox or Donkey from the stall, and lead it away to water it?" So ought not this woman, being a daughter of Abraham, whom Satan has bound - think of it - for eighteen years, be loosed from this bond on the Sabbath?*

I believe this story is an ideal scripture that points to the fact that a Christian (believer) can have a demon that brings sickness and infirmity. In the account we see that the woman had been crippled for eighteen years with a spirit of infirmity. We do not know how this spirit entered her, but one thing we do know is that it crippled her for eighteen long years. Jesus had compassion for her after suffering eighteen years in pain. I believe He still has compassion for people. The Bible tells us He is the same yesterday, today and forever. He is just looking for a suitable vessel to use on earth. Jesus is willing to heal the same today, for scripture tells us He has paid the price for the sickness and the sin of the whole world. I know of many people who have gone forward at a meeting to receive prayer for healing; sometimes they get small relief, but very often after a short time many are still the same. Many have been hurt and left the church when Pastors and Counsellors have said, "You do not believe or your faith is not good enough" leaving so many Christians feeling condemned, so much so that their faith can get weaker rather than stronger. If the sickness or infirmity is caused by a demon in the person's life' then a prayer for healing will not work. A demon cannot be healed, only cast out. There can be many entry points in our lives that give an opening to the demonic realm; the main entry point is sin. What we do, where we go, what we say, to whom we join ourselves. For example, generational sin is inflicted upon us by other people. Others include fear, trauma, doubt and unbelief of God's Word, all false religions and the occult.

Now this woman had her problem eighteen long years. What happened eighteen years ago? Some area in her life was open to vulnerability. The scripture does not tell us. We do know she did not have this problem at birth so something must have happened to allow the demon to enter.

A spirit needs a body to occupy in order to operate. When a spirit finds itself homeless e.g. after the person dies, it will search for a suitable place to dwell, preferably a close relative.

Numbers Ch 5 v 1- 2 states:

> *And the Lord spoke to Moses, saying: "Command the children of Israel that they put out of the camp every leper, every one who has a discharge and whoever becomes defiled by a corpse".*

Defiled or unclean (demonized). Many people especially in some cultures do this as a ritual, a superstition. I know it happened to me. I was told as a little boy to kiss or touch my dead Grandmother to stop me dreaming about her. Consequently I was brought up with an ungodly respect of superstitions all based on fear and lies. The Devil is the father of lies.

God says *'Do not fear'*. Job said, *'what he feared came upon him'*. Fear is the opposite of faith.

An example is a fifty-three year old man. Fifty of those years he had asthma. I asked him what happened fifty years ago. He said his family told him to kiss his Grandma who died so he would not dream about her. Fearfully he did so. She had asthma and now he had it. What happened – a spirit entered him. Consequently he received the same curse. After deliverance the man was healed. PRAISE GOD!

You see, people die but spirits do not. When the person dies the human spirit/soul leaves the body and goes to judgment – Heaven or Hell. The evil spirits or demons lie around the body in the lower heavens waiting to find a suitable home to live in, ideally in the family (Familiar Spirits). These are exactly what spiritualists call up when in a séance or spiritualist meeting. They are not the people they are contacting but the evil spirits representing the dead. They have knowledge about the person because they have been living inside them.

On another occasion I went to a special Church Leaders' Meeting where a few of the congregation were present. Later, as we enjoyed refreshments I found myself seated between two elderly ladies. In my evangelistic mood I approached them and asked if they were saved. "Oh yes," said one of the ladies.
"Well how do you feel now you are saved?" I said.
"Do you really want to know?" She said.
"Yes" I replied.
"My life is hell," she replied.
"Well I must say, I did not expect that answer," was my reply.
"My body is full of demons. I can feel them all over and inside me, and many of these Leaders and Pastors who I have spoken to tell me it cannot be so. They say, 'Now you are a Christian, you cannot be affected by evil, it is your imagination'."
"It is no coincidence that we are speaking." I replied, "My dear, I believe you. I have my wife and friends with me, if you wish us to

minister to you after the meeting we can do. I will first speak with your Pastor, as I know him, and believe him to be a man of God." We went to her home and started to pray in her room before we ministered to her. As we prayed in her room a voice came from the woman saying, "No".

This lady had been a medium before she became a Christian, visiting the spiritualist church nearly all her life. She had been intensively involved in 'transfiguration'. That is when a person invites a spirit to come into their life, and when it does, the people present can see the person's whole countenance change. These spirits become guides into the dark world of evil. This Lady had three such spirits, one a Red Indian, the second a Chinese man and the third an old lady. As we prayed she took on the countenance of these spirits as we challenged them to come out in the name of the Lord Jesus. Consequently, after two more sessions, the Lady was set free. Praise God she was able to really enjoy her latter years, fully knowing the love of Jesus in her life before passing on to be with Him forever.

I feel so privileged, by God's grace to be able to help these people. Praise God also for her Pastor who afterwards allowed me to teach and minister both to the Lady and also to the church. I have included a few true stories, hopefully to help the reader understand, that Jesus and His finished work on the cross is the only answer for all our needs. THANK YOU HOLY SPIRIT!

Satan is using his agents, like spiritualists and mediums, by causing them to lie and deceive vulnerable people. Especially those people who have gone through a trauma like the death of a loved one. Satan is using these people as his vessels because of their failure to understand the Word of God. The Devil is the master of deception. Remember, the worst deception is that which is closest to the truth. If we can not accept the scriptures as they are, how can we rely on any of the Word of God?

The Bible was written by the inspiration of the Holy Spirit, so one needs to have the Holy Spirit to understand what He wrote. Otherwise one will read the Bible with the wrong spirit and complain that it contradicts itself. This is why there are so many interpretations, contradictions and ideas which eventually become cults and heresies.

The infirm woman in the scripture had been bound by Satan for eighteen long years, yet she was a child of Abraham. Now sceptics will say that she was a Jew not a Christian. If we read Galatians Ch 3 v 7, it states:

Therefore know that only those who are of faith are sons of Abraham.

She was a woman of faith. She was a believer, with a spirit, that had caused the infirmity. Whether she was a Jew or not, was of no consequence. A Jew is not automatically a believer. In fact Jesus called the Jews, on one occasion, sons of the Devil. They protested and said, as recorded in John Ch 8 v 40 & 44.

"Abraham is our father, we are not illegitimate". Jesus said "But now you seek to kill me, a man who has told you the truth which I heard from God. Abraham did not do this" . . . "You are of your father the Devil and the desires of your father you want to do".

This woman believed God; and one day Jesus came along and released her. Today there are many waiting for Jesus to come along and release them, unfortunately if the Church is not open to God in this area, the captives still remain in bondage. I spoke to a lady who regularly attended a church. She had a problem with her hand; and after the medical profession had failed to solve the problem, she sought healing from an acupuncturist; she spent lots of money, only to get mild relief. When I told her that this was part of the New Age (Satan's counterfeit), she was sad that her church had not told her. Just as Pharaoh's magicians tried to copy Moses and Aaron by making their staffs become snakes, Satan uses New Age therapies to try to copy what God can do.

Exodus Ch 7 v8-12.

Then the Lord spoke to Moses and Aaron, saying, "When Pharaoh speaks to you, saying, 'Show a miracle for yourselves', then you shall say to Aaron, 'Take your rod and cast it before Pharaoh, and let it become a serpent.'" So Moses and Aaron went in to Pharaoh, and they did so, just as the Lord commanded, and Aaron cast down his rod before Pharaoh and before his servants, and it became a serpent. But Pharaoh also called the wise men and the sorcerers; so the magicians of Egypt, they also did in like manner with their enchantments. For every man threw down his rod, and they became serpents. But Aaron's rod swallowed up their rods.

If Satan can trick people into thinking they can be healed outside the church, then the teachings of Jesus are only just one idea, not the only way. In my experience, if people get either partial or seemingly total healing from the new age treatments, I have found that the problem was a spiritual problem in the first place and another spirit has now come in to cover over the original demon. Consequently the person is now left with more problems for the future. If the church believed the whole commission the medical profession would not be run off its feet.

Well praise God for the doctors, but Jesus is the Master Healer! He can do anything and everything! He laid his hands on the infirm woman and immediately she was loosed, an instant miracle. When a spirit has bound or put a person in a state of sickness and infirmity we should expect recovery to start to take place, sometimes instant, when the person is set free. This is why Jesus came, Luke Ch 19 v 10 states:

For the Son of Man has come to seek and to save that which was lost.

We read in the book of Acts Ch 10 v38:

How God anointed Jesus of Nazareth with the Holy Spirit and with power who went about doing good and healing all who were oppressed by the Devil, for God was with him.

When we read the scriptures we see that God always seems to anoint men and women, not some sort of denomination or movement. In fact, the synagogue ruler was more interested in keeping the rules of his religion rather than he was with seeing the woman healed. I wonder if today people are kept in bondage because the church officials would sooner keep their religious ordinances and denominational doctrines rather than humbling themselves before Almighty God and show love and compassion (not sympathy) for the people in need. Jesus called the ruler of the synagogue a hypocrite because He knew what was in the ruler's heart, Jesus inferred that the synagogue ruler had more compassion for his Ox or Donkey than he had for the woman; Jesus knows the condition of all our hearts.

In John Ch 2 v 23-25, it states:

> *Now when He was in Jerusalem at the Passover, during the feast, many believed in His name when they saw the signs that He did. But Jesus did not commit Himself to them, because He knew all men and had no need that anyone should testify of man, for He knew what was in man.*

Can He fully commit Himself to us today? After all, it is only He who knows what is inside us. He knows whether we believe in what He says or not, for He is the One who will ultimately say "well done my good and faithful servant". How can He say that, if we have not been faithful to the commission which He gave us? The scripture tells us these people saw His miracles and believed in His name, but Jesus would not commit Himself to them. He could not trust Himself to them. Can He trust us today? He knows what is in our hearts. He knows if we believe. He knows if we have a real desire for people to be set free. He knows whether we are more interested in ourselves or our ministry, rather than fulfilling the commission that He has called His believers to do.

I do hope and pray that we will not be found wanting when He brings us to account for the way we have treated His mandate for our lives.

After He had healed the woman, Luke Ch 13 v17 says,

All his adversaries were put to shame.

Jesus was also testing the hearts of the Synagogue rulers. The very ones who thought they understood the Word of God were put to shame, but whatever they thought or said, Jesus ignored for the sake of this woman who loved Him. She was hoping that one day God would heal her. I believe that one day God will set those free who really put their trust in Him. Jesus will come to their rescue, the word rescue sums up the deliverance ministry. If that is you, then you will know there is an answer for your life. If you have been prayed for, to be healed, and it has not worked, maybe there is a spirit causing the problem? A spirit cannot be healed, but when the demon is cast out, healing can take place. Your deliverance was all paid for at Calvary when Jesus paid the ultimate price. For He said 'It is finished', at that point Satan's power was broken. We have to implement that freedom by fulfilling the commission.

4. TAKING TERRITORY

Many people need much persuasion to change the ungodly teachings and traditions of their predecessors, who have taught in the past that believers cannot have a demon. As we continue, we will hopefully understand that this is not the case.

Matthew Ch 15 v 21-28. states:

> *Then Jesus went out from there and departed to the region of Tyre and Sidon. And behold, a woman of Canaan came from that region and cried out to him, saying, "Have mercy on me, O Lord, Son of David! My daughter is severely demon-possessed." But He answered her not a word. And His disciples came and urged Him, saying, "Send her away, for she cries out after us". But He answered and said, "I was not sent except to the lost sheep of the house of Israel". Then she came and worshipped Him, saying "Lord help me!" But He answered and said, "It is not good to take the children's bread and throw it to the little dogs". And she said, "Yes, Lord, yet even the little dogs eat the crumbs which fall from their masters' table." Then Jesus answered and said to her, "O woman, great is your faith! Let it be to you as you desire". And her daughter was healed from that very hour.*

We know, as we read the scriptures in the Old Testament, that the Canaanites were involved in all types of demonic practices, such as sexual immorality, witchcraft, spiritualism, child sacrifices, sorcery and all the abominable practices that God hated. Now we do not know whether this child was involved herself, but scripture seems to imply that the mother was still her guardian, she could have been affected by the sin of her ancestors. When a baby is born he or she is not perfect. Children do not need to be taught how to be naughty, but they do have to be taught to be good. There are many scriptures on how to raise a child, most of them in the Book of Proverbs, the book of Wisdom.

Here are a few

Proverbs Ch 20 v 11:
Even a child is known by his deeds, by whether what he does is pure and right.

Proverbs Ch 22 v 6:
Train up a child in the way he should go, and when he is old he will not depart from it.

Proverbs Ch 29 v 15:
But a child left to himself brings shame to his mother.

As children are a product of their parents, they are therefore spiritually attached to both father and mother. They will inherit strengths and weaknesses and family traits (blessings and curses), and will be spiritually affected by at least four generations. That means that it is possible, at least thirty people have a link to the new born. That does not mean that God does not love the children, or that they are not already under God's protection until they come to an understanding of sin.

In the Ten Commandments the second one explains that God is a jealous God, visiting the iniquity of the fathers on the children to the third and fourth generations of those who hate Him. The fact is, if we do not totally follow His ways, then we by our own actions give Satan a right into our lives and that of our descendents which can leave devastating effects on lives.

Deuteronomy Ch 23 v 2-3 states:
One of illegitimate birth shall not enter the assembly of the Lord; even to the tenth generation none of his descendants shall enter the assembly of the Lord.
An Ammonite or Moabite shall not enter the assembly of the Lord; even to the tenth generation none of his descendants shall enter the assembly of the Lord forever.

So we see that there is a curse down to ten generations for illegitimacy and child sacrifice which was the requirement of the gods of the nations of Ammon and Moab (Chemosh and Moloch). At least two thousand and forty-six people along with all their spiritual connections can be affecting the life of the unborn child in these cases. These nations would have illegitimate children then have them sacrificed.

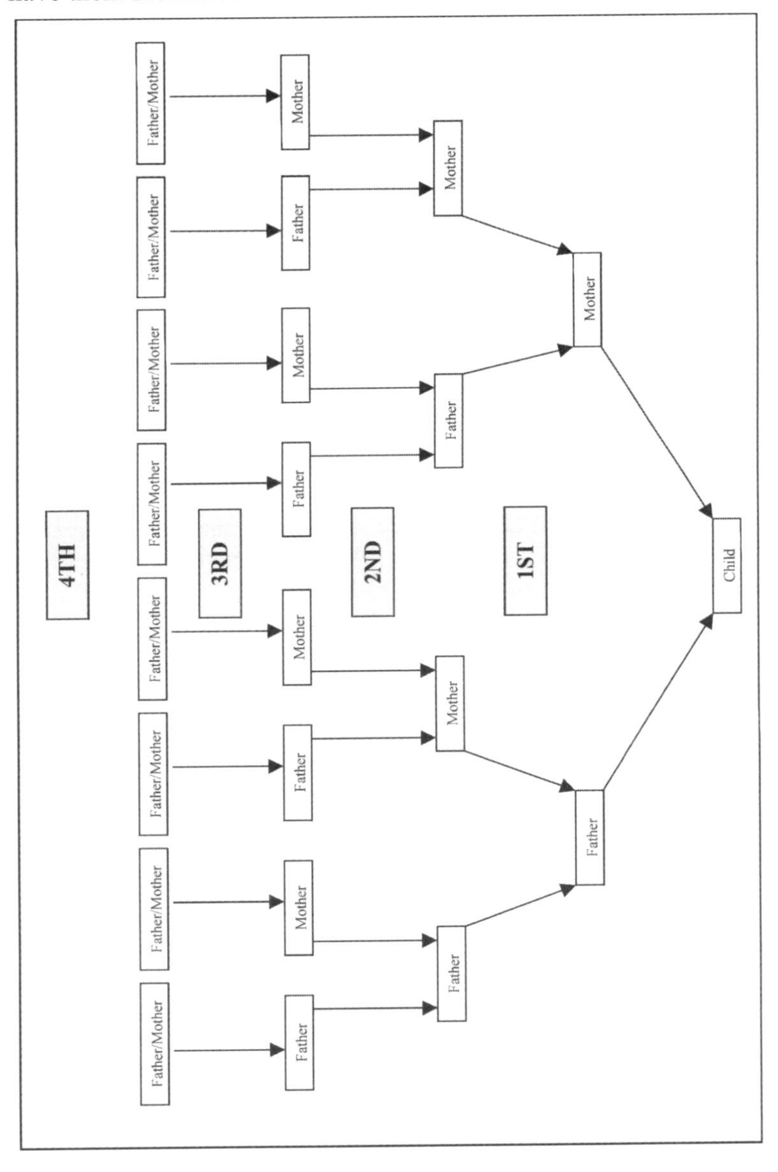

What seems worrying is when the Lord uses the word forever in verse 3. Further on in the chapter we see why, because these people hired a man named Balaam to put a curse put on the children of God.

Deuteronomy Ch 23 v 5:

Nevertheless the Lord your God would not listen to Balaam, but the Lord your God turned the curses into a blessing for you, because the Lord your God loves you.

This lines up with the scripture in Romans Ch 8 v 33:

Who shall bring a charge against God's elect? It is God who justifies.

So if we are obeying and trusting in the Lord then nothing can, by any means, harm us.

At God's perfect time in history, Jesus was born.

If we follow the ancestral line of Mary in the account in Luke Ch 3 we can see that there were 19 generations of blessings from Zerrubbabel the son of Shealtiel, to Jesus.

If we follow Joseph's ancestral line in the account in Matthew Ch 1 we can see that there are ten generations of blessings from the same man Zerrubbabel a man chosen by God (the book of Ezra Ch 3---). Even though Jesus was not the son of Joseph, He had to be brought up in a God fearing family, Joseph was His guardian until He became of age, God had to chose the right man, just as He had to chose the right woman, for the greatest job given to any human being at that time.

However, Jesus is the one who can set us free from any generational curse, if we come to Him.

In the account of the Canaanite woman's daughter, it states that, she had a demon and it was obviously a problem for her to be able to enjoy a happy life. The mother had the faith to believe Jesus could do something. The story seems to imply that it was the sin of the mother that caused the child to be demonized because she said, "have mercy on me," but that we cannot be sure. However we do know that the sins of our parents and ancestors have a direct influence on the next generation.

A lady came for ministry who was living in England but as a teenager came from the Far East. Her whole family was part of Taoism, into which she was taken as a baby. One day when she was young she was taken by her mother to see a Taoist priest, for healing, because of eczema on her arms. The priest was a man who ministered with a woman's voice. The priest cut his tongue and with the blood wrote a prescription on some yellow paper and dissolved it in water and told the young girl to drink it. The eczema improved. Many years later this teenager then moved to England. She had not been in touch with her mother for many years. Unexpectedly she received a letter from her mother telling her to stop seeing this particular man of a certain nationality. Astounded and worried the girl could not understand how her mother could know? The mother had been able to obtain information about her daughter through the priest's witchcraft. The girl being a new Christian did not know what to expect but she requested prayer. A spirit came right from the pit of her stomach as we broke the control and spiritual connection with the priest. PRAISE GOD. Jesus is the deliverer!

Ezekiel Ch 16 v 4 states:

> *And as for your nativity, on the day you were born your navel was not cut, nor were you washed in water to cleanse you; you were not rubbed with salt nor wrapped in swaddling cloths.*

The scripture speaks about our cord not being cut from birth. Now of course the cord is cut physically, otherwise we would still be attached to the placenta from the mother. Here the scripture is saying that we were not cut spiritually from our ancestors. Here is a place where all Christians need to be spiritually separated, ideally. After all, in the light of our ancestry it is impossible to be born perfect, as the Bible says that not one is perfect.

Jesus answered the woman, not a word. It can be a lonely time when you cry out to God and you feel He is not listening. Jesus was listening to her cry, if fact He did say that "He was only sent to the lost sheep of Israel".

Even when Jesus sent out the disciples, He only told them to go to the lost sheep of the House of Israel and not to go into the way of the Gentiles or enter a city of the Samaritans. Yet we all know that His ultimate plan was for the whole world, but He had not revealed this to anyone at that time. Nevertheless this woman never gave up. She cried out and begged Jesus to heal her little daughter. She reached-out for what God had not revealed at that time. That was Faith. The woman had no positive word from Jesus until she called Him "Lord". Jesus saw her heart and He commended her for her great Faith. Even though Jesus had not revealed His plan for the world, He could not ignore a heart that called out to Him with the faith that she had. If we have the Faith, He has the Power to do it. The disciples wanted to get rid of her. Through fear this can happen today. People who know they need ministry have been ignored and even ejected from meetings because they have screamed when the Holy Spirit was present. Yet when the disciple Philip ministered we see a different scenario as we can read in Acts Ch 8 v5-8

> *Then Philip went down to the city of Samaria and preached Christ to them. And the multitudes with one accord heeded the things spoken by Philip, hearing and seeing the miracles which he did. For unclean spirits, crying with a loud voice came out of many who were possessed; and many who were paralyzed and lame were healed. And there was great joy in that city.*

Notice there was great joy in that city. When the Lord is present with His miracles and the Holy Spirit is allowed to move and all arguments and church politics are pushed to one side and the focus is on Jesus and Him alone, great joy comes in to the meetings for the living God is amongst us.

The Lord's next two statements to the woman in Matthew Ch 15 are very profound. The first one can be found in verse 24,

"I was not sent except to the lost sheep of the house of Israel"

This implies that the children of God can have a problem. The woman called Him "*Lord*" and cried "*help me*".

The next verse we need to focus on is in verse 26 of the same passage. Jesus then said,

> *"It is not good to take the children's bread and toss it to the little dogs,"*

Jesus is implying it is not right to give to little dogs (meaning little gentiles), that which should only be given to the children. She agreed and said, *"True Lord, yet even the little dogs eat the crumbs which fall from their master's table."* She believed that even the smallest blessing would be good enough if it came from God. She certainly recognized who Jesus was and was willing to make Him 'Lord'. "O Woman," Jesus said, "great is your faith let it be as you desire". The little girl was healed from that very hour. Here Jesus is explaining that the ministry of deliverance is only for believers, not for unbelievers. It is for Born Anew believers, not for the world. It is to prepare the body of Christ for the Bridegroom, to cleanse and sanctify, to make us effective in the Kingdom, and to give us life in abundance.

It is not really beneficial casting demons out of unbelievers if they are not prepared to come to Christ and makes Him Lord as they are already in the Devil's kingdom, until they repent. Jesus said to the Jews in John Ch 8 v 24,

> *"Therefore I said to you that you will die in your sins; for if you do not believe that I am He, you will die in your sins".*

Therefore if a person wishes to accept Christ but cannot because of demon possession, (that means spirit, soul and body). That is possession (which means ownership). A <u>Christian cannot be totally possessed</u> because God lives in their spirit. In a situation like this Jesus gives us the authority to bind and loose. So we have authority in Jesus to bind Satan's influence, whilst the person is led to Christ.

I was called to minister one evening at an outreach meeting and a man came for prayer. It was obvious to me that he needed major deliverance. So I first thought I must make sure that he was a Christian. He said he wanted to accept the Lord. To me it was imperative that he made a personal commitment to Christ. So I led

him in a prayer, and he repeated the words after me, when I said, "I accept Jesus to be my Lord and Saviour."
His response was "I accept Satan as my lord and saviour." This happened three times. So I asked him, "Do you have difficulty saying the words?"
"Yes, every time I try; that's what I say," he replied.
So I bound the spirit. Then he successfully accepted Christ. Praise God!

Then after further prayer, he was set free.

In Matthew Ch 18 v 18 it states:

> *"Assuredly, I say to you, whatever you bind on earth will be bound in heaven, and whatever you loose on earth will be loosed in heaven".*

In Matthew Ch 12 v 43-45 it states:

> *"When an unclean spirit goes out of a man, he goes through dry places, seeking rest and finds none. Then he says, 'I will return to my house from which I came.' And when he comes, he finds it empty, swept, and put in order. Then he goes and takes with him seven other spirits more wicked than himself, and they enter and dwell there; and the last state of that man is worse than the first. So it will be with this generation".*

In this passage we can see how evil Satan is. Not just seven other spirits but seven worse spirits will enter that person. We can see how Satan hates all mankind. If we cannot do a person good we should never willingly by our actions do them harm by casting out a demon from an unbeliever. There is so much confusion in the body of Christ regarding demons living or not living in a Christian that many have no real understanding even though they have been in ministry for many years. The Devil is the instigator of confusion.

If there is not a spirit in the person it cannot be cast out.

To me it is quite obvious that the evil one does not just leave upon salvation otherwise why did Jesus say 'drive' (with force) 'them out'? Some will say that a Christian can only be oppressed. If that is so, why '<u>Drive them out</u>'?

Paul cast out the spirit of divination from the slave girl in Acts Ch 16 v 16,

> *Now it happened, as we went to prayer, that a certain slave girl possessed by a spirit of divination met us, who brought her masters much profit by fortune-telling. This girl followed Paul and us, and cried out, saying, "These men are the servants of the Most High God, who proclaim to us the way of salvation". And this she did for many days. But Paul, greatly annoyed, turned and said to the spirit,*
>
> ***"I command you in the name of Jesus Christ to come out of her"***

The spirit came out of her. She was speaking the truth and letting everyone know about God's plan of salvation. Paul was not happy; in fact he spent several days discerning the spirit that was working through her. There was something that Paul was not comfortable with. Then one day he turned around and commanded the spirit to come out of her. If it came out, it was obviously in before. Not oppressing her but controlling her. Her owners were furious because she had lost the ability to tell fortunes and make them money, so they dragged Paul and Silas off to the Authorities and had them flogged, then put into prison. Paul had concluded that this woman was a believer otherwise the cast out spirit would have returned with seven of its friends, in which case her owners would have been rejoicing because Paul would have done them a favour. It can be the same with us today.

People can be in Church; saying the right thing, doing the right thing, but with an unclean spirit working through them. People that are saved can have controlling spirits, bringing disunity and endeavouring to bring in their own agendas to try to manipulate the situation for their own aims. Manipulation, control, intimidation, domination are all signs of witchcraft working in the Church, in families and their relationships. The object of all witchcraft, black or white is all the same, it is for someone to have power over another. This can even be in all sorts of relationships, even from Pastors in the Church, because of their inferiority or inadequacy to be able to deal with the person in a loving way. Jesus was always able to deal with every situation. His instructions are in the Bible. His life was directed by His time alone with God.

A pregnant mother living in England visited a fortune-teller to find out if the baby would be a girl. The fortune-teller confirmed her wish and all was fine, the new born baby girl was born healthy, grew up and eventually was married. This young wife, was invited one day by her neighbour to a W I (Women's Institute) meeting to see a guest clairvoyant from America. Knowing nothing about the young wife the clairvoyant told her some truths about her family. As the family grew the lady moved to another house, only to find that she had moved next door to a white witch. This new neighbour then presented the lady with a gift for the expected but yet unborn child she was carrying. The baby, a boy, was born healthy they believed, but later was found to have a colon disorder, which caused him much discomfort as he grew up. He became a great concern for the doctors and specialists who were divided as to whether to intervene with surgery or not.

However, the young mother received prayer for herself, to be cut off from all witchcraft and was set free when the spirits dramatically left, even back to the time that the spirit had entered in her whilst she was in her mother's womb. The young mother was prayed with again, this time in proxy for the child who was miles away at that time. The spirit was commanded to come out of the child and come out through his mother, again a powerful deliverance and the child was set free and wonderfully healed. He is a healthy, young man now serving the Lord full time. Praise God for Jesus. ALLELUJAH!

5. BREAKING FREE

Mark Ch 5 v 1 – 20 states:

Then they came to the other side of the sea, to the country of the Gadarenes. And when He had come out of the boat, immediately there met Him out of the tombs a man with an unclean spirit, who had his dwelling among the tombs; and no one could bind him, not even with chains, because he had often been bound with shackles and chains. And the chains had been pulled apart by him, and the shackles broken in pieces; neither could anyone tame him. And always night and day, he was in the mountains and in the tombs, crying out and cutting himself with stones. When he saw Jesus from afar, he ran and worshipped Him. And he cried out in a loud voice and said, "What do I have to do with You, Jesus, Son of the 'Most High God'? I implore you by God that you do not torment me." For He had said to him, "Come out of the man, unclean spirit!" Then He asked him, "What is your name?" And he answered, saying, "My name is Legion; for we are many." Also he begged Him earnestly that He would not send them out of the country. Now a large herd of swine was feeding there near the mountains. So all the demons begged Him, saying, "Send us in to the swine, that we may enter them." And at once Jesus gave them permission. Then the unclean spirits went out and entered the swine (there were about two thousand); and the herd ran violently down the steep place into the sea. So those who fed the swine fled and they told it in the city and in the country. And they went out to see what it was that had happened. Then they came to Jesus, and saw the one who had been demon-possessed and had the legion, sitting and clothed and in his right mind. And they were afraid. And those who saw it told them how it happened to him who had been demon – possessed, and about the swine. Then they began to plead with Him to depart from their region. And when He got into the boat, he who had been demon-possessed begged Him that he might be with Him. However, Jesus did not permit him, but said to him, "Go home to your friends, and tell them what great things the Lord has done for you". And he departed and began to proclaim in Decapolis all that Jesus had done for him; and all marvelled".

Jesus made a special journey over to the other side of the lake. It seems the only reason was to help this man who had problems. He was prepared to go for just one, not long before this He was ministering to the multitudes. This just shows me how He knows everything, He knows our troubles and problems and His ministry, fantastic as it is, is also very individual. He cares for us all. The country of the Gadarenes, whose capital was Gadara at that time, was south east of the Sea of Galilee. Just before all this happened Jesus was asleep in the boat with His disciples, they were confronted by a storm on the sea. The disciples had to wake Him up.

Sometimes we let Jesus go to sleep in us, and not until we are in a mess do we wake him up, either in our own lives or in the church. This is not the time to let the Holy Spirit go to sleep. Jesus rebuked the storm. Then all was calm and they landed straightway on the seashore. I believe this storm was inspired by evil powers, in fact it must have been or He would not have had to rebuke it. This also reveals to me that Satan can affect this atmosphere in the Lower Heavens. Gadara was the capital of the area of land that belonged to the tribe of Gad, one of Jacobs' sons. In the Old Testament Moses and the children of Israel went to war against the Amorite kings namely Sihon, King of Heshbon and Og King of Bashan who was at Ashtoreth. It is this part of the area of land called the Gadarenes; which originally belonged to the Amorites, the land which Moses shared out between the tribes of Gad, Reuben and the half tribe of Manasseh.

Numbers Ch 32 v 1-5 states:

Now the children of Reuben and the children of Gad had a very great multitude of livestock; and when they saw the land of Jazer and the land of Gilead, that indeed the region was a place for livestock, the children of Gad and the children of Reuben came and spoke to Moses, to Eleazar the priest and the leaders of the congregation, saying "Ataroth (Ashtoreth), Didon, Jazer, Nimrah, Heshbon, Elealeh, Shebam, Nebo, and Beon, the country which the Lord defeated before the congregation of Israel, is a land for livestock, and your servants have livestock." Therefore they said "If we have found favour in your sight, let this land be given to your servants as a possession. Do not take us over the Jordan".

Moses was displeased with these tribes at this point. The reason was that they wanted to settle for second best. These tribes were more interested in their own desires rather than to stay together as a nation and to finish the work that the Lord had instructed; that was to move right into the Promised Land and to take possession of it. What about us today, do we only want Jesus on our terms and only do what we think is right, or are we willing to obey Him even if we stand alone?

Are we willing to get true unity of the Holy Spirit, working as one man with one mind and one heart for the Gospel of Jesus Christ?

The Church should speak with one voice believing the word of God just as it is; and not compromise to suit others.

Numbers Ch 32 v 14-15:

"And look! You have risen in your fathers' place, a brood of sinful men, to increase still more the fierce anger of the Lord of Israel. For if you turn away from following Him, He will once again leave them in the wilderness, and you will destroy all these people".

It was because of their forefathers' rebellion that the children of Israel were made to wander forty years in the wilderness until they had all died. Only Joshua and Caleb survived. Now a similar situation had arisen. Moses was implying that their failure to obey would have a direct impact on the rest of the nation. That is a sobering thought. Where does that put the Church of Jesus Christ today? Could it be that unbelief and disobedience have a direct impact on other Christians throughout the world? What about our local Christian fellowships? Eventually these three tribes agreed to join their brothers and go to war and to cross over the Jordan River, after making sure that their families and livestock could stay behind in the land which eventually became their possession. Following this the land still was the home of every ungodly practice. It is possible to settle for second best, but the Lord does not wish this for his children. He has paid too high a price for us to stay under Satan's influence. The price has been paid for our healing, body, soul and spirit. Further on in the scriptures we find that King Solomon set up high places for the goddess Ashtoreth (which means Flocks and Riches).

2 Kings Ch 23 v 13:

> *Then the King defiled the high places that were east of Jerusalem, which were south of the Mount of Corruption, which Solomon king of Israel had built for Ashtoreth the abomination of the Sidonions, for Chemosh the abomination of the Moabites, and for Milcom (Moloch) the abomination of the people of Ammon.*

We read in 2 Kings Ch 23 v 4 where King Josiah defiled the high places of the pagan practices, and then he burned them. He also commanded the High Priest, as well as the other priests and doorkeepers, to bring out of the temple of the Lord, all the articles that were made for the demon gods which Solomon allowed into the temple. Ashtoreth was the goddess of sexual lust and perversion. Ashtoreth is also known by the name Astarte or Asherah, sister and wife of Baal (the god of the storm and rain). No wonder the disciples had a problem getting to the other side of the lake. This story can be found in Mark 4 v 35-41. After Jesus calmed the storm, he went ashore; the demonized man immediately came from out of the tombs to meet Him. He was cutting himself with stones, unwittingly trying to remove the demons. This happens in some religions today. They may try all ways to remove the demons. It is not unheard of today, of people cutting/abusing and inflicting pain upon themselves, for similar reasons. I personally have counselled many who have either slashed their wrists with a knife or such like because it temporary relieved tension in their bodies. Unfortunately this practice actually made

them worse. It is only the authority of the name of The Lord Jesus Christ that the demons have to obey and flee. Some religions actually cut the faces of the women to ward off evil spirits. Rather than ward them off, this practice will let them in. On one occasion the Pharisees said Jesus was casting out demons by Beelzebub (the prince of demons).
Jesus answered in Matthew Ch 12 v 27:

> *"If I cast out demons by Beelzebub by whom do your sons cast them out".*

Once I was challenged, about delivering Christians. My reply was "what about the commission that the Lord gave to His disciples?" The answer was, "get them saved and then they cannot have a problem with demons." My reply was "If that is true, then why does the scripture in Mark Ch 16 v 15-18 not just say save the people. Also why are some Christians still experiencing problems after they have been saved?"

To understand this scripture you have to realize that demons do speak through people and you need to discern which voice is from the man and which is from the demons. When the demonized man saw Jesus he ran and fell on his knees and worshipped Him. It was the man who fell on his knees and worshipped God, not the demons. The man obviously recognized who Jesus was. The man shouted, "I implore you, do not torment me". This man was already tormented out of his mind with the demons, and now that God has come on the scene the man is more frightened, for he probably knew what God and His wrath could do to him.

Luke Ch 12 v 4 -7 states:

> *"And I say to you, My friends, do not be afraid of those who kill the body, and after that have no more that they can do. But I will show you whom you should fear: Fear Him who, after He has killed, has power to cast into hell; yes I say to you, fear Him! Are not five sparrows sold for two copper coins? And not one of them is forgotten before God. But the very hairs of your head are all numbered. Do not fear therefore; you are of more value than many sparrows".*

The demons can do a lot of harm, yet nothing in comparison to what God's wrath can do. This man realized this and he knew that he deserved a greater penalty than what he had at that time.

God had the power to cast him into Hell.

This man expected God's wrath but instead he received mercy.

Many today do not know the loving kindness of our Father in Heaven. Jesus did not come to torment this man, but to heal and release him. This a wonderful picture of Salvation? For what we have done we deserve Hell and torment and I know for my actions I deserve the same, but our Wonderful Saviour forgives, heals and delivers with his love and compassion. This man is showing us the power of repentance. Jesus had already spoken to the unclean spirit to come out of the man, so we have two characters (like schizophrenia), the man and the demon. Jesus asked him (the demon, not the man) what his name was. "My name is Legion, for we are many," the demon replied. The man's name was not Legion for the scripture says they were many. The demon begged Jesus not to send them out of that country.

The demons were under Satan's control and felt they had a right to be in that country. The only right they have is when mankind gives it them through sin.

> *"Send us to the swine, that we may enter them," the demon begged.*

For many years I have often wondered. 'Why Jesus even listened to the demons or even agreed to what was asked for? Was Jesus limited in power? Did He have to make a deal with the Devil? Was Jesus weak at this point? Did He agree with the demons' request because He thought the man had been tormented enough? Or was Jesus one step ahead of the Devil and the Lord knew the Evil One's cunning, lying tricks? Well I believe that the latter was just the scenario. Just like at Calvary, the Devil thought he had won. Jesus and all our sins were nailed to the tree with Him, then He died, and was buried and then raised from the dead.

THAT WAS WHEN JESUS NAILED THE DEVIL TO THE TREE

That is why Jesus whilst on the Cross said, in John Ch 19 v 30,

"It is finished!".

Jesus agreed to the demons' request, the demons came out of the man and went into the swine, about two thousand pigs, but then something happened that the Devil did not expect. All the swine went running over the end of the cliff and into the sea where they were drowned. The man was totally healed and in his right mind. But why did Jesus allow the pigs to die? When God made all Creation, He said that, *"It was VERY GOOD,"* including the pigs. So did He really have to sacrifice two thousand swine? After the law the Lord pronounced swine as unclean animals. Could He not have stopped the swine being killed? Was this the only way to get rid of the demons? I believe this happened to pronounce judgment on the swine. We have a God of compassion (for the man) and a God of judgment (for the sin). Heaven is real, so is Hell and damnation. I believe Jesus was fulfilling the Law written in Leviticus Ch 20 v 15.

If a man mates with an animal, he shall surely be put to death, you shall kill the animal.

To me this seems the only explanation; otherwise there would be no reason to kill the swine. Also the man knew that God was all knowing, which is why he begged Jesus not to torment him. All through the ministry of Jesus, God was showing to the Pharisees and the people that Jesus truly was the Messiah. At one time Jesus said:

Matthew Ch 5 v 17,

"Do not think that I came to destroy the Law or the prophets. I did not come to destroy but to fulfil."

When the woman was brought to Him who was caught in the act of adultery, the fulfilment of the Law was stoning to death.

His miraculous healings were to show that God had no favourites.

The blind, the deformed, the leprous, those with broken limbs and anyone with any defect, were not allowed by God's Law to do the work of a priest by distributing the sacrifice offering to the people. They could eat it, but not distribute it. That is why Jesus did many miracles on the Sabbath day. The man who had dropsy, healed on the Sabbath in a Pharisees home. The paralyzed man, who was lowered through the roof, was healed on the Sabbath. The woman with the spirit of infirmity was healed on the Sabbath. The man in the synagogue with a withered hand was healed on the Sabbath. The woman who had been bleeding for twelve years, the raising from the dead of the synagogue ruler's little daughter, two blind men healed, a demon possessed mute man healed and set free, all were healed on the Sabbath day. This proved that Jesus was the Lord of the Sabbath. These healings particularly upset the Pharisees who relied on the keeping of the Law even though they could not keep it themselves, and had no compassion for those who they could expose who had broken the Law.

Whenever the Law was broken it always brought a spiritual consequence, it is the same today. When the Law of God is broken, there is a sentence to pay. The sentence is the fulfilment of the Law. Jesus was the fulfilment of the Law. He took on the sentence and paid the debt for our sin. What a beautiful Saviour. All His miracles proved that He was a God of compassion for those who came to Him.

God instructed Moses to tell the children of Israel not to defile themselves with the abominations and ordinances of the people of the Land of Canaan. All types of sexual perversions were some of the practices they committed. When people do this; their lives are wide open to the demonic realm.

I believe the man in the story had been committing the sin of bestiality. Things have not changed even to the present day, but like other sins, God is able to forgive and the blood of Christ is able to cleanse and to set free. The demons wanted to go back to where they had came from, maybe to lure others into the same trap. This man now repented, (worshipped Jesus) so Jesus set him free. As he was from the area of the Gadarenes as we have said earlier, from the tribe of Gad, the man would have known the penalty for his sin which was death. The man recognized that Jesus was God so expected for the sentence to be carried out, yet he received mercy, Jesus set him free. Afterwards the man went all through the area telling what Jesus had done for him.

In the book of James Ch 2 v 13 it states,

Mercy triumphs over judgment

The demons needed a body and thought they would be at home in the pigs, maybe to lure others into the same sin. This is why we must allow God to rid us of all Satan's demons in our life. The scripture tells us "we must take the plank out of our eye before we can remove the speck out of someone else's eye." For example, how can you deal with a spirit of lust in someone if you have it yourself? We as Christians must be constantly coming before the Lord to see if there is any wicked way in us as spirits are looking for a home to live in, whether in a pig or in a human. People have sometimes needed deliverance after they have been involved in setting others free, mostly because they are living in two camps. God expects us to be one hundred percent for Him, unfortunately some people think they can seek God one day and read and believe their horoscope the next day, or visit the new age alternative therapy healers the next day. Or even pray to God one day and say the oaths and rituals of the Masonic Lodge etc the next day.

One day God, One day the Devil.

There is a story in the Old Testament in 2 Kings Ch 4 about the prophet Elisha, he returned to Gilgal (the place where Joshua had put the stones out of the Jordan River). Gilgal should have been a place of blessing instead there was a famine. The sons of the prophets were also there. Elisha told the servant to make some stew, but the servant put in some wild gourds, which poisoned the stew. They cried out, *"O man of God there is death in the pot."* So Elisha fixed it by putting flour in the stew.

This is exactly what happens when a Christian gets mixed up with other spirits, we get poisoned. For instance, the Mormon Church read the Bible (which is good because God's Word brings life). Unfortunately they also read and accept the Book of Mormon which is poison (that will bring death).

The Bible tells us we cannot drink the cup of the Lord and the cup of demons also. The man in the story was living in the area of the Gadarenes, whose goddess was Asthoreth, (Goddess of immorality and sexual perversion), all in the land of Canaan.

Canaan was the son of Ham. The son who went into his father's tent when his father was drunk. This we can read in Genesis Ch 9 v 20 – 25.

And Noah began to be a farmer, and he planted a vineyard. Then he drank of the wine and was drunk, and became uncovered in his tent. And Ham, the father of Canaan, saw the nakedness of his father, and told his two brothers outside. But Shem and Japheth took a garment, laid it on both their shoulders, and went backward and covered the nakedness of their father. There faces were turned away, and they did not see their father's nakedness. So Noah awoke from the wine, and knew what his younger son had done to him. Then he said: "Cursed be Canaan: a servant of servants He will be to his brethren".

Noah knew what his son had done to him. What could Noah have known if his son had only looked at him? It seems as though the brothers were so disgusted that they could not even look upon the incident. Take in comparison the account in Genesis Ch 19 v 30 – 35:

Then Lot went up out of Zoar and dwelt in the mountains, and his two daughters were with him; for he was afraid to dwell in Zoar. And he and his daughters dwelt in a cave. Now the firstborn said to the younger, "Our father is old, and there is no man on the earth to come into us as is the custom of all the earth. Come let us make our father drink wine, and we will lie with him, that we may preserve the lineage of our father." So they made their father drink wine that night. And the firstborn went in and lay with her father, and he did not know when she lay down and when she arose. It happened on the next day that the firstborn said to the younger, "Indeed I lay with my father last night; let us make him drink wine tonight also, and you go in and lie with him, that we may preserve the lineage of our father." Then they made their father drink wine that night also. And the younger arose and lay with him, and he did not know when she lay down or when she arose.

After reading about all that had happened with Lot and his daughters, yet both times Lot being drunk neither saw or even knew anything about it. In both situations both became drunk. So what did Noah see? What did Ham do to his father Noah to make him see something? Well if we look further we see Noah did not curse Ham himself, but it was Ham's son Canaan that Noah did curse. Canaan's border of land extended to Sodom and Gomorrah. The sin reached its completeness at Sodom and Gomorrah so God destroyed both cities.

Many today are suffering with a curse because of what our ancestors have done. Some people feel today that they have been born homosexual. Well even if that were true, it does not mean that God made them like it. God made Adam and Eve, Male and Female and perfect. Sin entered the world and now we are of a fallen race. God can heal and deliver that person out of Satan's grip, if they wish to. One sin will lead to another, a man may get involved in gay relations, and then that could lead him into the occult and witchcraft. The Devil may even try to destroy him so much so that he may even go all the way to try to make himself a woman. Jesus can set that person free. Often the problem stems from rejection by those who should provide the most security, either by accident or intentionally even whilst in the womb. Or the parents were longing for a boy, buying all the toys etc even before the birth and the child was born a girl, but with male tendencies. Obviously this problem can affect both genders.

A person may have been abused by a person of the same gender and the abused person even may detest themselves for the actions even blaming themselves, yet they continue in this pattern. This is a demon. I know of cases where a father was abused in this way, the father did not become homosexual but unfortunately the next generation did receive the spirit and continued the abuse.

Leviticus Ch 18 v 22 it states:

You shall not lie with a male as with a woman. It is an abomination.

This sin in the Old Testament law was a sin punishable by death. People are not put to death today, but they certainly receive a curse. This I believe is the reason why God stopped the three tribes (the three sons of Noah) building the Tower of Babel, not because they would reach to Heaven, because that was impossible, but because some were blessed and some were cursed.

Genesis Ch 11 v 3-4 it states:

> *Then they said to one another, "Come let us make bricks and bake them thoroughly." They had brick for stone, and they had asphalt (the word slime is used in AV Bible) for mortar. And they said, "Come, let us build ourselves a city, and a tower whose top is in the heavens; let us make a name for ourselves, lest we be scattered abroad over the face of the whole earth".*

So how can the same sin be acceptable in the Church of Jesus Christ today and for the people involved and those agreeing with it, be part of God's Church? It is the same as joining with all religions worshipping their gods, or their ways to their gods in interfaith meetings when the Bible says those who are Born Anew will be blessed and those who are not, God's curse remains on them? This is a situation that really needs to be prayed about if your have been Born Anew.

1 John Ch 5 v 12 states:

> *He who has the Son has life; he who does not have the Son of God does not have life.*

They tried to build the Tower of Babel with bricks not stone. These people were trying to reach up to Heaven with man made bricks. It is the same today. The Church of Jesus Christ cannot build the Kingdom of God with works of the flesh only by the Holy Spirit. The Church today may be trying to build with things that are not natural, types of relationships that God has cursed. Christians should seriously consider their role in the body of Christ and who and what they are relating to. These tribes were using slime to hold the bricks of the Tower of Babel together. The Church I feel must be careful only to build with the right ingredients, things that are pure. They were using slime for mortar. Resentment/unforgiveness/bitterness and selfish ambitions and all filth are regarded as slime. The Bible tells us Love must be sincere, otherwise the Church will be in danger of going into Captivity.

1 Corinthians Ch 3 v 10-17 states:

> *According to the grace of God which was given me, as a wise master builder I have laid the foundation, and another builds on it. But let each one take heed how he builds on it. For no other foundation can anyone lay than that which is laid, which is Christ Jesus. Now if anyone builds on this foundation with gold, silver, precious stones, wood, hay, straw, each one's work will become manifest; for the Day will declare it, because it will be revealed by fire; and the fire will test each one's work, of what sort it is. If anyone's work is burned, he will suffer loss; but he himself will be saved, through fire. Do you not know that you are the temple of God and that the Spirit of God dwells in you? If anyone defiles the temple of God, God will destroy him. For the temple of God is holy, which temple you are.*

It seems we can not only build on things that are seemingly of not much worth (hay, wood, straw,) but things that we think are good and valuable (gold, silver, precious stones,)

Only the work that is the Will of God will stand the fire.

After all, who are we working for? Who is the Boss? How can anything eternally good come from something opposite to the instructions which Almighty God has declared? No doubt the Man in the Tombs was under the influence of the evil of others that had found a way to trap him and to keep him in state that he found himself, before Jesus came into the situation. Just look at the state of our world because Jesus is not allowed on the scene today. The people of the town of Gadara in the story asked Jesus to leave. Rather than rejoice because the man had been set free and healed they were upset. Probably they did not like to see their riches going into the sea and be drowned, or was it that Jesus had exposed their sin? Jesus would not let the man follow Him but instructed him particularly to testify what God had done. So he went around the whole region and did just that. That is why testimonies are very powerful as God is no respecter of persons and He does not show favoritism.

6. KNOWING YOUR ENEMY

Micah Ch 7 v 8 it states:

> *Do not rejoice over me my enemy; when I fall I will arise; when I sit in darkness, The Lord will be a light to me.*

Many people often betray, lie, cheat and talk about us, but when it comes from those closest to us, it hurts all the more. The pain, disappointment, rejection and betrayal can feel like a knife in our hearts.

Micah Ch 7 v 6 states:

> *A man's enemies are the men of his own household.*

I believe this scripture has a deeper meaning than our natural household.

The book in the Bible entitled the Song of Solomon calls these *"the little foxes that spoil the vine".* These little foxes, these enemies of ours, are Satan's landmines that he can have hiding away and sometimes we can be totally unaware that they are there, until they rear their ugly head. It is then that they need to be caught. These little foxes can make a real mess and sometimes bring upon us pain and disgrace. We need to come before the Lord to show us if there is any wicked way in us. Probably my favourite song is an old hymn by Edwin Orr the first verse is

> "Search me O God, and know my heart today;
> Try me O Lord, and know my thoughts I pray:
> See if there be some wicked way in me,
> Cleanse me from every sin and set me free."

Notice the hymn writer asks the Lord to do seven things,

1) search him
2) know his heart
3) try him
4) know his thoughts
5) expose wickedness
6) cleanse me
7) set him free

2 Corinthians Ch 5 v 16 highlights this.

Therefore, from now on, we regard no one according to the flesh.

The Bible also likens our bodies (which we regard as our temples) as a house. A house in the natural is where you often keep your belongings, the things that you have worked for, the things that are special to you. Jesus gave a parable about the wise man building his house upon a rock.

In Matthew Ch 7 v 24 it says:

"Therefore whoever hears these sayings of Mine, and does them I will liken to a wise man who built his house upon a rock".

Again we read in Luke 11 v 21 – 26:

"*When a strong man, fully armed, guards his own palace (house), his goods are in peace. But when a stronger than he comes upon him and overcomes him, he takes from his armour in which he trusted, and divides his spoils. He who is not with Me is against Me and he who does not gather with Me scatters. When an unclean spirit goes out of a man, he goes through dry places, seeking rest; and finding none, he says, "I will return to my house from which I came." And when he comes, he finds it swept and put in order. Then he goes and takes with him seven other spirits more wicked than himself, and they enter and dwell there; and the last state of that man is worse than the first."*

Both God and the Devil liken their dwelling to be a house. There is a battle for our house, (our body and our soul). Our spirit hopefully, has been regenerated by God's Holy Spirit.

The latter is an ideal scripture to show the Church that we should be filled with the Holy Spirit, so that when the demons are expelled and they try to return from where they came from, they find 'No Vacancies' on the door.

Hebrews Ch 4 v 12-13 states:

> *For the word of God is powerful, and sharper than any two edged sword, piercing even to the **division of the soul and spirit**, and of joints and marrow, and is a discerner of the thoughts and intents of the heart. And there is no creature hidden from His sight, but all things are naked and open to the eyes of Him to whom we must give account.*

The Holy Spirit comes to our spirit when we get "Born Anew". The Word of God now severs between our spirit and our soul, as we touched on in an earlier chapter, so He can reveal to us the real person that we are.

We need to get to know ourselves by inviting the Holy Spirit and God's Word into every situation of our lives (into our temple – into our house); then we will get to know our enemy. What is in us? Only we know ourselves, and what we don't know, God knows. He will do what He wills and we should do what we can. First of all, God commands all to repent, then by our own choice we should seek baptism by full immersion and the infilling of the Holy Spirit given by God.

We are all a product of our ancestors, from whom we need deliverance (already covered in an earlier chapter). All our ungodly relationships and the ties we have with other's souls from our ungodly past need to be broken and be set free from spiritually. Soul ties can be Godly and ungodly. Godly ones are ties that we have to our parents, brothers and sisters and spouses. These can become ungodly when the relationship is not according to God's ideal, along with every relationship that does not line up with the word of God, emotionally, sexually, physically either voluntary or abusively. Scripture says in Genesis Ch2 v 24. *When two become together they become one.* Divorce does not set you free spiritually, and in this fallen world that we live in, our ungodly partners can be joined to many more, with the scenario that we could be joined spiritually to most of the town or even further. Some might be witches, harlots or whatever. Illness can be caused by the joining to others from soul ties.

Hosea Ch 4 v 6 states:

My people are destroyed for lack of knowledge

Isaiah Ch 57v 1 states:

The righteous perishes, and no man

takes it to heart

These scriptures are warnings for believers. Satan is so deceiving God's people that many of His righteous ones are perishing because of lack of knowledge of God and His Word. So many Christians think that their old activities such as involvement in witchcraft, visiting the spiritualist, playing on the Ouija board or visiting the Palmist, do not matter when they have repented (going once is enough to bring about a curse). If they truly repent God will forgive. It is the affect of the sin on a life which is the problem – Sin leaves consequences.

A lady came for prayer. She had stomach problems and had much surgery. She also had problems in the mind. Her father was a Freemason. The oaths and rituals of Freemasons bring curses on them, their spouse and children, even down to the fourth generation. The third degree oath is about 'having their bowels ripped open' and another is about cursing of the mind, as well as the many rituals that they go through. This girl needed major prayer deliverance, but the Lord is able and He set her free. Whilst in ministry the Lord gave us words of knowledge. One was lesbian, another was abortion. On the pronouncement of these words, spirits manifested but didn't leave. So we naturally thought that a specific prayer of repentance was needed first, however she had not been so involved. This became confusing until the Lord gave a word of knowledge 'Blood Pact'. The truth is, when she was a small girl she did a blood pact, like many have done. This lady and her friend pricked their fingers and joined themselves together (soul tie). When this was prayed about, the demon of abortion and perversion screamed and left her. The Devil is cunning and he is the master of trickery. He has had many years of this. It is only in Jesus that we can beat him. PRAISE GOD FOR HIS GIFTS!

After the spirits had left, then the lady remembered and said, "Oh this childhood friend was a lesbian and she has had an abortion".

For instance, I wonder if those involved in Freemasonry and all the other ritualistic organisations would actually say all the oaths, go through all the rituals and call upon all the pagan gods if they realized that they were cursing their unborn grandchildren. Satan is the master of deception. If only people would turn to Jesus for their answers in life.

In the light of this true story, just look at the devastation that is being passed down to the children born after an abortion. The present news is that the British Government backs the right for doctors to keep abortions for the under sixteen-year-olds in the dark without even a right for the parents to know. Yet at five weeks old the baby's finger nails can be detected, at twelve weeks the baby is moving his or her legs. At the moment of conception there is a child.

Matthew Ch 2v 20-21:

"Joseph, Son of David, do not be afraid to take to you Mary your wife, for that which is conceived in her is of the Holy Spirit, and she will bring forth a son, and you shall call his name JESUS."

The reason why the Devil loves abortion is because in that womb there could be a man or woman of God. There is so much anger towards the murderers of little children from all society today, or even recently when a notorious doctor killed hundreds of his patients, but what about the first degree murders of millions of innocent children in the womb? The perpetrators are allowed to get away with it, without even receiving a prison sentence. The sad thing is many others suffer through their rebellion.

Isaiah Ch 57 v 7-9 states:

On a lofty and high mountain You have set your bed; Even there you went up to offer sacrifice. Also behind the doors and their posts You have set up your remembrance; For you have uncovered yourself to those other than me, and have gone up to them; You have enlarged your bed, where you saw their hand. You went to the king (Moloch. NIV version), with ointment, and increased your perfumes; You sent your messengers far off, and even debased yourself even to Sheol.

Moloch was the God of child sacrifice. This spirit is still working today in abortion. The scripture explains that these people God was speaking to, had uncovered (sacrificed) to someone other than the Lord. The Devil comes to steal, kill and destroy, but Jesus came to give us life.

This lady in her innocence as a child obviously did not understand the consequences of her actions. Satan is a destroyer and he never warns you beforehand about tragic circumstances arising from lack of knowledge of God's word.

There is always a consequence to the sin we commit. King David committed adultery with Bathsheba the consequence was, she became pregnant. Then King David had Uriah the Husband of Bathsheba deliberately put into battle where he would face certain death. David tried to hide his sin but God saw it. David begged for forgiveness, God forgave, but the consequence was that the baby died.

Sexual Immorality today can often lead to murder, namely abortion. If God does forgive the persons involved, there is the consequence of a dead baby, also there is the trauma that the parents go through. Many are tormented, and need deliverance from the spirit of murder, guilt and grief.

In the old hymn, the composer Charles Wesley got it right in the words 'O for a thousand tongues to sing'. In verse three it says,

**'He breaks the power of cancelled sin,
He sets the prisoner free'**.

The sin has been cancelled but the power behind the sin needs breaking in Jesus name.

We need to be careful what we allow into our minds. Videos and television particularly, as our minds are very delicate and can be affected, especially at an early age. I understand this all too well as a spirit entered my mind and tried to control my thought pattern for over twenty five years, giving trauma and fear. This resulted in my taking medication on and off for many years. I had a fear of sleeping and my life was in total despair. I cannot bear to think where I would be or what I would have done if I had not had a faithful God fearing and prayerful Mother. At one stage another voice spoke through me which was quite weird. Successful in the world, but confused mentally and emotionally, until the Master set me free. The medical professions sometimes give tape recordings for the patient to listen to whilst asleep, obviously believing that whilst a person is asleep they can still receive messages. If that is so, what happens when one falls asleep in front of the television and an unsuitable programme comes on which would normally be switched off? It may be filled with swearing and blasphemy or witchcraft, violence or a sexual perversion, which all too often is on the television these days. There are instances in the world today where some people have watched videos or programmes which include violence or that are of a sexual nature, and they have then reinacted what they have seen into real life, even murders. This can be seen on a lesser scale even in television soaps, where people react as though it is real life. So what is the reason why this affects so many people? We (mankind) are a product of where we have come from, who we relate to, what we do and where we go. When our minds are open to such videos etc, and remember, we all are spirits living in a body with a soul. Our minds are delicate and can receive influences from the mind of the person who made the film, at that time or the person starring in the film. You can be totally ignorant of what spirit is guiding that person. I speak from experience, after I received the demon; it affected me so much that my thinking changed as a result of the hypnotic influence of the horror film. We need to guard our minds and particularly those of the children.

Another one of our enemies is our tongue. We need to watch our tongue when we talk about ourselves and others. The Bible tells us in James Ch 3 v 8-9

> *But no man can tame the tongue. It is an unruly evil, full of deadly poison. With it we bless our God and Father, and with it we curse men, who have been made in the similitude of God.*

So we need to be careful not to say negative words about ourselves or others or we may be putting a curse on the same. Jesus never spoke anything negative, so why should we? If I look at my own life, I can see that when I have spoken negatively, it is usually because I have wanted to pull others down, so I could be looked upon more favourably. I can see that this attitude stems from inferiority and insecurity. Subtly I would be trying to manipulate the situation for my own ends. This in the light of scripture is a form of witchcraft so we must be constantly aware not to give the Devil an opening. Many are living under a curse of negative words spoken by others. Freedom comes through repentance and forgiveness including forgiving ourselves. Scripture tells us we should love our neighbour as we love ourselves. The degree with which we love ourselves shows the degree we love our neighbours. Not a vane love, but responsible caring love. Some say they cannot love themselves, maybe through guilt they cannot forgive themselves. Yet the Lord is willing, so we should also be willing. Spiritual snobbery must be repented of, when I use this term it is referring to the situations where it is possible not to preach to friends, because if one does and they get saved the new convert will be on the same spiritual footing as oneself. Yet you may call them friends, this is a contradiction of terms, and not love.

Matthew Ch 18 v 34 -35 states:

> *And his master was angry, and delivered him to the torturers until he should pay all that was due to him, so My heavenly Father also will do to you if each of you, from his heart, does not forgive his brother his trespasses.*

If we are unwilling to forgive as God forgives then the scripture says we will be handed over by our Father in Heaven to the tormentors (Demons). We hurt ourselves by our unwillingness to forgive. This is why I said;

we must love ourselves and forgive everyone including ourselves.

The apostle Paul recognized this in 2 Corinthians Ch 2 v 5 –11.

> *But if anyone has caused grief, he has not grieved me, but all of you to some extent - not to be too severe. This*

punishment which was inflicted by the majority is sufficient for such a man, so that, on the contrary, you ought rather to forgive and comfort him, lest perhaps such a one be swallowed up with too much sorrow. Therefore I urge you to reaffirm your love to him. For to this end I also wrote that I might put you to the test, whether you are obedient in all things. Now whom you forgive anything, I also forgive. For indeed I have forgiven anything, I have forgiven that one for the sakes of the presence of Christ, lest Satan should take advantage of us; for we are not ignorant of his devices.

This man that the apostle Paul is talking about was earlier the subject of controversy in 1 Corinthians Ch 5 for the Bible tells us he was involved in incest with his father's wife. Whether it was his actual mother by birth the Bible is not specific, yet the consequences were still the same. He was a product of his father, so the man in question had an incestuous relationship through the soul tie, even if it had been his stepmother. The Church expelled him but later he repented as we must do of all sin. Paul knew if the Church did not forgive him from their heart and reinstate him, comfort him and to show their love to him then the church would be handed over to the tormentors, to the Devil. I wonder how many church congregations have been handed over to the demons because of unforgiving, a lack of love and no restoration. No wonder we see so much illness and powerlessness and the lack of the presence of the Holy Spirit in the apparent Church today.

Matthew Ch 6 v12 states:

And forgive us our debts, AS we forgive our debtors.

With the measure you use it will be measured to you. Matthew goes on to say in verses 14-15:

For if you forgive men their trespasses, your heavenly Father will also forgive you. But if you do not forgive men their trespasses, neither will your Father forgive your trespasses.

The apostle Paul was not ignorant of Satan's schemes so neither should we be.

Paul said he had forgiven for the presence of Christ, which shows that the presence of Christ can be lost in the Church even though we sing the same songs, preach the same messages, give the same tithes or change leadership. All this will not set the Church free from the influence of demons. We must forgive, comfort, love, and reaffirm the people involved.

7. MINE-SWEEPING

We need to check our armour, making sure there are no holes in it, so the enemy's arrows do not strike through. 'Mine Sweeping' in the context of this chapter is about sweeping the house clean of the garbage we have collected. Garbage attracts and encourages infestation by parasites and infectious diseases.

Some things we collect or buy or wear, are not glorifying to God in fact they directly glorify the evil one. In the occult dictionary it says a symbol is a representation of a higher order. In other words it represents something greater than what it actually is. It is inviting that spiritual power into and around wherever it is displayed. It is just like the high places that King Solomon set up south of the mount of corruption (Mount of Olives 2 Kings Ch 23 v13).

1 Kings Ch 11 v 4-8 states:

> *For it was* so, *when Solomon was old, that his wives turned his heart after other gods; and his heart was not loyal to the Lord his God, as was the heart of his father David. For Solomon went after Ashtoreth the goddess of the Sidonians and after Milcom the abomination of the Ammonites. Solomon did evil in the sight of the Lord, and did not fully follow the Lord as his father David. Then Solomon built a high place for Chemosh the abomination of Moab, on the hill that is east of Jerusalem, and for Moloch abomination of the people of Ammon. And he did likewise for all his foreign wives, who burned incense and sacrificed to their gods.*

A married couple started a prayer meeting in their home. One night the man heard supernatural movements in his house. Every night this was happening and on one particular night he found blood on the bathroom door. This was very worrying, and could find no natural explanation. Reluctantly, having tried to clear up the matter alone, eventually he felt he should mention it to his wife. I was called upon to investigate the matter. As we walked around the house we were led by the Holy Spirit to look at certain objects that they had placed around the room. My eyes were drawn to a brass unicorn (a mythological being) prominent in the new age imagery. The man then destroyed the object and we prayed in the house, commanding the demons to leave. There was not a problem ever again. THANK YOU JESUS!

Deuteronomy Ch 7 v 25 – 26:

> *You shall burn the carved images of their gods with fire; you shall not covet the silver or gold that is on them, nor take it for yourselves, lest you be snared by it; for it is an abomination to the Lord your God. Nor shall you bring an abomination into your house, lest you be doomed to destruction like it. You shall utterly detest it and utterly abhor it, for it is an accursed thing.*

THE WORD OF GOD NEVER LOSES ITS' POWER.

In the Bible the only place where the Lord God told the Jews to wear a symbol was in Deuteronomy Ch 6 v 4 – 9:

> *Hear, O Israel: The Lord our God is one. Love the Lord your God with all your heart and with all your soul and with all your strength. These commandments that I give you today are to be upon your hearts. Impress them on your children. Talk about them when you sit at home and when you walk along the road, when you lie down and when you get up. Tie them as symbols on your hands and bind them on your foreheads. Write them on the door posts of your houses and on your gates.* NIV translation of the Bible.

The present day Orthodox Jews do exactly this. The Lord told them they must have His commandments in their hearts. There was even a teacher of the law who agreed with Jesus about these commandments and about Loving Your Neighbour as yourself. Yet Jesus said to him "*You are not far from the Kingdom of God*" Mark Ch 12 v34. Without faith in Jesus Christ, even believing in all the commandments, it still did not earn the teacher of the law a place in the Kingdom.

When the children of Israel were in the wilderness they spoke against God and Moses, so God sent fiery serpents amongst the people and many died. The people acknowledged their sin and begged Moses to ask the Lord to take away the serpents. God did not take away the serpents, but instead He told Moses to make a bronze serpent and put in on a pole and lift it up high. Anyone who was bitten by the serpents only had to look upon the symbol and they would be healed. This can be found in Numbers Ch 21. This symbol had been preserved for over seven hundred years and was still around at the time of King Hezekiah, until he broke it into pieces because the people were worshipping it. The story can be found in 2 Kings Ch 18 v 4.

Jesus referred to this in the gospel of John Ch 3 v14:

> *"And as Moses lifted up the serpent in the wilderness, even so must the Son of Man be lifted up"*

The Devil is the master of trickery he will abuse, defile, or pervert anything if it can get us to even glance away from lifting up Jesus.

'Symbols' that represent their gods.

Today Christians wear symbols like the so called Star of David (six pointed star). In Stephen's great speech in Acts Ch 7 v 43 he says:

> *"You also took up the tabernacle of Moloch and the star of your god Remphan, images which you made to worship; and I will carry you away beyond Babylon".*

It is no more than the star of Moloch (the god to which the idolatrous nations used to sacrifice the children). Stephen recognized this; after he told them the truth he was stoned to death. This star is also the symbol on the Master Masons' jewels, whose god is Lucifer (Satanism in disguise). Other symbols are the Menorah, seven-branch candlestick; this symbol was also an ancient Babylonian symbol, also used as a symbol in Freemasonry and is displayed in the temples of the Masonic Lodges. The deceptive issue is that this symbol is supposed to represent the one that God instructed the Jews to make in the Old Testament. Yet it cannot be reproduced today exactly as God originally designed. The Jewish authorities have painfully tried to do so. What then do the ones represent that people wear today and display in their homes? Bearing in mind the Devil always tries to copy God.

Sometimes Christians can be led by the wrong spirit even when they try to promote Christianity. One such example is the symbol that many people use on Christian giftware, namely the yellow smiley face (Smile – Jesus loves you). Little do most people understand that it is the symbol of Acid House, the drug culture movement. The symbol daubed tabs of LSD (Acid) and Ecstasy pills also T-shirts, general paraphernalia etc. The only one who is smiling, is the evil one, when Christians are snared.

Occultists, spiritualists and many unbelievers wear crosses some with no idea what the cross was all about. But many occultists use them in rituals. The Ankh (a cross with a circle over the top bar is a satanic symbol. Celtic crosses (a cross with a circle in the centre) can be bought in any witchcraft shop. The Lord says, *"It is by their fruits you will know them"* not by symbols. When people are prayed for after removing symbols, nearly every time they get a release from the powers that they represent. Some say a symbol does not matter; it is what is in your heart that counts. I agree it is what is in your heart that counts, so why do you need a symbol.

Baptism is a symbol, yet very powerful. The water is not special but Jesus says if we are buried with Him we shall be raised with Him. Romans Ch6 v5.

Communion is a symbol, again very powerful, only Bread and Wine, yet scripture tells us in 1 Corinthians Ch 11 v 30:

For this reason many are weak and sick among you and many sleep (died).

Because they had taken Communion in an unworthy manner people were sick and even died, yet it was only bread and wine. It was a symbol of what it represented. It still represents the Body and the Blood of Our Lord Jesus Christ. "What! A symbol has power over life and death?" It takes some believing! But not really when you realise that it is the power behind the symbol which can either bless or curse.

We need to be alert spiritually to what we wear. Jewellery, does it glorify God? Who had it beforehand? What were they involved in?

A man came for prayer who is now a Christian, but before, he used all types of talismans round his neck to draw down the demonic rulers into his life. This man was in a very bad state spiritually, and it was only after concentrated prayer over a few weeks that he was finally set free in Jesus' name. Some people have had devastating consequences by not understanding the demonic influence behind the symbols that they have and wear.

We are bombarded with a rise of tattoo and body piercing shops on the high streets of our towns; many promoting and giving glory and honour to Satan, all invoking curses on the persons lives. Some parents even take little babies to the occult tattoo parlours to be defiled.

Leviticus Ch 20v 28:

> *You shall not make any cuttings in your flesh for the dead, nor tattoo any marks on you: I am the Lord.*

Many people have felt wonderful release when they have had the curse broken of the tattoos. Sometimes people have not been delivered from their involvement like the playing on the tarot cards or martial arts until their tattoos have been renounced and prayed over.

Cuttings of the flesh for the dead is the same as body piercing which is being done on and in nearly all parts of the body that can be physically got to. If the Lord wished mankind to have a lip ring or a tongue stud etc. we would have been born with one. Like a spiritualist or medium in a séance will call up the spirits of the dead, so does body piercing give an open door to the world of evil? You may think that takes some believing, well here is a true story.

One night a man came to our church in a terrible state. Mentally unstable – he took a knife into a police station and demanded to be locked up. He eventually finished up in a mental hospital for many months; at one stage many staff and doctors could not hold him as he was ripping doors and door frames out with his bare hands. Finally he was injected with medication to control him and was under constant care and supervision. After release he came with his girl friend to church where he was prayed for. He obviously needed deliverance. He was wearing three earrings one of which was a very sturdy one. I asked him why he had that one. His answer was he had done a pact with two other men and they all had a similar earring. One man was now dead through an accident, but before he died he was in and out of the mental hospital, the other man has been in and out the mental hospital ever since. This earring was taken out; in fact all the earrings were taken out. The pact was renounced and repented of. The spirit and the soul ties were broken, three demons were cast out and the man was back in his right mind. Similar to the man in the tombs. Last year I had the privilege to marry the couple and now they are regular church members. JESUS is the same Yesterday Today and Forever!

Another time I was visiting a Pentecostal Church and the Pastor did not accept that a Christian could have a demon. A young lad was prayed for at the front of the church. He was shaking and manifesting because a demon was being brought to the surface. It would not leave, so the Pastor asked if I could help. The Lord directed me to the earring that he was wearing. The young man took out the earring and with the prayer of deliverance the shaking stopped; he knew he was set free. Praise the Lord!

Judges Ch 8 v 24:

> *Then Gideon said to them, 'I do have one request of you, that each of you would give me the earrings from his plunder'. For they had gold earrings, because they were Ishmaelite.*

Gideon had just won a mighty battle, three hundred men against as many as the sand on the seashore. The Ishmaelites were and still are unbelievers to the gospel of our Lord Jesus Christ. The body piercing practice and tattooing, is against the Word of God.

Many people through vanity and pride are proud of their tattoos and body piercing, and may not wish to accept this teaching because they feel they are permanent, so they accept them as friends. God said He will set us free from our enemies. So firstly their attitude to these so called friends has to be changed. God said He will set us free from our enemies, but not our friends. To be set free, repentance needs to come first, and then seek the Lord for deliverance from those enemies. You will find He is always faithful to His promise, that He came to set the captives free.

I, myself, was convicted when I read a book on blessings and curses. It mentioned tapestries with dragons on. Well, I had similar things. In my lounge I had two large Chinese rugs with two dragons on each, all with five toes (Emperor Dragons). Because they were expensive and I had only just acquired them, I decided to take them back to the shop. I asked my wife if, when she went shopping, she could take them back to the shop and choose two others. Praise God for our wives. She said "I cannot take them back if they are cursed, the shop keeper might sell them to someone else and they will be cursed." So she was hearing from the Lord.

I decided to take them out of the house and put them in an outbuilding. For weeks I passed by them, trying to put them out of my mind. Then one day I bought some paraffin and set fire to them. Amazingly, shortly after, the telephone started to ring, and people not known previously to me, were asking me to pray for them. Many asked if they could come to my home for prayer. I now understand that the Lord was not happy to work in my home whilst I had objects that were glorifying to Satan (The dragon is a symbol of Satan in The Book of Revelation). Also it has been an object of idolatrous worship for centuries.

We need to ask ourselves if we have objects in our homes that have spiritual connotations, things that we have collected or which have been passed down the family line. These can include new or second-hand objects, for example furniture, rings, bracelets, necklaces, pictures, videos, CDs, records and books all connected with the supernatural and the occult. Wind chimes are other objects I have had to destroy. I have already explained about talismans. Do not even covet the silver or <u>gold on them</u>. So I personally will not even melt it down to make it into something else, just destroy. Pictures of Jesus or even Jesus on the Cross, sorry, pictures of a man on a cross. How do we know it is Jesus on the cross or the picture? Have we got a photo of what He looked like? It could be the thief on the cross that went to Hell. I ask you 'Who is it'? We need to burn and destroy all articles like brown scapulars, statues, idols, rosary beads and any religious artefacts. All idols and ornaments of false Gods (like Buddha) need to be destroyed.

The Bible tells us in 1 Timothy Ch 2 v 5:

For there is one Mediator between God and men, the Man Christ Jesus.

A Godly man who is a widower has a large family. He has a nice property but could find no peace in the house. He was never happy in the house since his wife died and he began to detest the house. His wife was a Christian before she died but before they were married she was a fortune-teller. One day I went to visit and he told me how he felt. As I looked around the room my eyes were focused on a photo. I promptly said "That photo needs to be burnt." He replied, "I cannot do that, it is a photograph of my wife. All the children have one." Then I looked at another photograph of him, his wife and children. I said, "No that is your wife, she is now married to you, under your authority which the Bible tells us is God's order for mankind. The first photo was your wife before you were married and at that time she was a fortune-teller. She is even wearing the fortune-teller's scarf. Would you have a photo of some famous clairvoyant in your house?"

"No! Never!" was his reply. "Then you need to burn it" I said. When the man did this and also other photos connected to the ancestors with an occult connection, we prayed, and there was a new presence come into the room as the Holy Spirit was now there and happy to be in the Man of God's house. Well that is not the end of the matter. The Lord at the same time was convicting his sons and daughters in different parts of the country to do the same. Supernatural experiences were happening in the homes of the sons and daughters through the photographs. Many came for prayer and the witchcraft control over the family was broken. CHRIST JESUS IS LORD!

We need to burn all books with occult connections and all books sacred to other religions and secret societies. All objects, ornaments and regalia of Freemasons, Orange order, Buffaloes and every organisation that needs an oath to join. Remember a promise or oath is the same thing, Jesus said in Matthew Ch 5 v 37,

> *"But let your Yes be Yes and your No, No. For whatever is more than these is from the evil one".*

I have found that if we have to argue about anything in the Bible our hearts are not right with God. We should not let the evil one have a foothold into our lives. Many people felt oppressions leave when they have had a good spring clean. Be thorough, it will be worth it.

The apostles brought the same teaching to the early Christians. If it was right for them, it certainly is right for us.

Acts Ch 19 v 19 states:

> *And also many of those who had practiced magic brought their books together and burned them in the sight of all. And they counted up the value of them, and it totalled fifty thousand pieces of silver". So the Word of the Lord grew mightily and prevailed.*

They burned them in the sight of all. It was a good thing for everyone watching because they could see the repentance by their actions. It would have also stopped the tongues wagging about whether the people in question were prepared to accept the apostles teaching. Photographs of ungodly relationships need to be burnt including all pornographic material, and anything that keeps you connected to the old life of sin. These are abominable to God.

When people demonstrate their faith by their actions the word of the Lord will grow mightily and it will prevail. When something has cost us a great lot, either in time, effort or money, we cherish it more than if it comes cheap. Our salvation did not come cheap, it cost God His only Son so that He could get many sons. If it cost God His only Begotten Son. He knew our deliverance was not going to be easy and without a great cost.

That is the difference with our faith and all other religions. They only demand that the believer obeys certain rituals or laws. The Lord will tell you if you need to do some mine-sweeping? The Lord will convict you if there is anything that needs to be done. If you respond in obedience you will feel at peace with God in spite of the cost. Our conscience tells us if we allow the Lord to rule in our lives.

When we look at some of our church buildings we see demonic figures called Gargoyles on the outside. Supposedly they were put there to ward off evil spirits. Rather than ward off, I believe that they are a kind of talisman to draw powers towards them. Most cannot be broken off, because this world system has put a conservation order on the building. No wonder there are so many spiritual problems in the apparent church. How can a gargoyle ward off evil spirits? Are the church architects trying to say the gargoyles will frighten the demons away? Jesus said *'Satan will not drive out Satan'*.

Matthew Ch 12 v 26 – 28 states:

> *"And if Satan casts out Satan, he is divided against himself. How then will his kingdom stand? And if I cast out demons by Beelzebub, by whom do your sons cast them out? Therefore they shall be your judges. But if I cast out demons by the spirit of God, surely the kingdom of God has come upon you".*

Jesus goes on to tell us to drive them out (with force), evict them or expel them. The reason that they do not just leave is that they have worked hard to get there. With the Spirit of God which He has placed in each Born Anew believer, the Lord has given us the authority to deal with them in His name.

8. KNOWING YOUR AUTHORITY

There is a place we can get to in Christ, in which we can be aligned to the right position to receive His blessings on our lives, as we seek Him and believe His word. If we only knew who we were in Christ maybe the Church as a whole would be more powerful. It is one thing to read it, but another to believe it.

Colossians Ch 1 v 26 – 27 demonstrates this:

The mystery which has been hidden from the ages and from generations, but has been revealed to His saints. To them God willed to make known what are the riches of the glory of this mystery among the gentiles: which is Christ in you the hope of glory.

The apostle Paul speaks about a mystery that has been hidden. It has been God's plan throughout the generations, since the fall of man. The mystery is Christ in you the hope of glory. Christ in us, what a wonderful reality. If Christ is in us, just look at the power and authority that God has invested in each believer. Jesus said in his own words in

Matthew Ch 28 v 18,

"All authority has been given to 'Me in heaven and on earth".

He now lives in them that have been '<u>Born from Above</u>.' That means all authority in Heaven and on Earth is given to you if you fit into that category. The Church has this authority. For a time in my life as a Christian I was not really grasping the full meaning. When we use loosely the words 'Born Again' it seems to suggest we just have another chance, as I wrote in Chapter one. The 'Born Anew' experience fits in with other scriptures like John Ch 1 v 12 – 13:

But as many as received Him, to them He gave the right to become children of God, to those who believe in His name: who were born, not of blood, nor of the will of the flesh, nor of the will of man, but of God.

We have been born of God (born from above). Jesus was born of the Holy Spirit; He came into a body of dust, and became a man, out of the womb of a woman. We were originally born of man, but then we were "Born Anew of the Holy Spirit" when we repented of our sinful life, and accepted Christ Jesus. When Jesus was thirty years old He was baptized and the fullness of the Holy Spirit came upon Him like a dove. When we get baptized by full immersion as Jesus did, the Lord promises to us the Holy Spirit as He also did for the first disciples. The scriptures confirm this in Acts Ch 2 v 38 – 39:

> *Then Peter said to them, "Repent, and let every one of you be baptized in the name of Jesus Christ for the remission of sins; and you shall receive the gift of the Holy Spirit. For the promise is for you and to your children, and to all who are afar off, as many as the Lord our God will call".*

When I first came to the church, I had no idea what to expect. I knew things were not right with me, I would never have thought that I would share my secret problems with anyone.

Because I was a self-made business man, my arrogance and pride would not let me. I trusted no-one and had little interest in anyone outside of my inner family circle. When I was told that God had gifts for me and He wanted me to receive them now, I started to get interested because I was also a greedy person. So I said to myself, "You mean that Almighty God has gifts for me, I do not know what they are but I want them and I intend getting them whatever it costs me."

Little did I know that it would cost me my greed, my pride, my arrogance and my very life?

Notice in the scripture it says, *"To all who are afar off"*". The children that are *afar off* are the Church of Jesus Christ today and tomorrow. It seems the only one who had an excuse for not being baptized was the thief next to Jesus on the cross to whom Jesus said, "*Assuredly, I say to you, today you will be with Me in Paradise*". The act of baptism is the burying of the old life. This thief was going out of this life. If it is at all possible, a believer must be baptized <u>after</u> a confession of Christ as his or her saviour.

Romans Ch 6 v 3-5 states:

> *Or don't you know that as many of us as were baptized into Christ Jesus were baptized into his death? Therefore we were buried with Him through baptism into death, that just has Christ was raised from the dead by the glory of the Father, even so we should walk in newness of life. For if we have been united together in the likeness of His death, certainly we also shall be in the likeness of His resurrection.*

Jesus said to the Jews that He was '*from above*'. John Ch 8 v 23.

The scriptures say we cannot continue to sin if we have been "Born of God." There has to be a change in our thinking and our lifestyle. If we start to believe and understand that we have been 'Born from Above' it may change our whole outlook to the gifts and blessings that the Lord has for all His children. Not to make us proud, but to make us like Jesus.

If you are a Christian you need to seek the Lord for the gifts He has labelled with your name on. We all must reach out for the high calling that He has for our lives. To be in God's will is the finest life we can ever have, it is worth all one has to give up. We must make a decision to love Him with all of our heart.

Jesus said to His disciples in Matthew Ch 5 v 14.

> *"You are the light of the world".*

If we are the light of the world why is the world so dark?

We need to get our batteries recharged and let the light shine. It is the responsibility of every Born Anew believer to witness for his or her Saviour. If you are full of light you will shine and the light will have to shine out, but if you are full of darkness only darkness will come out.

The Church must start to believe who they actually are. We have been brought back from the dead, WE ARE ALIVE. When you go out witnessing you are witnessing to dead people (dead in their trespasses and sins). We have been called to raise the dead, that can be physically and spiritually as well.

Just imagine being around Jesus, two thousand years ago when He stopped the funeral procession at a town called Nain so He could raise the little boy up from the dead, and then lift him out of the coffin. Imagine the situation today. All the funeral cars are in line, flowers all around the coffin, the cars are just going down the High St of the local town. Jesus steps out from off the pavement, He flags down the hearse. He says something like, "Remove the flowers, take the coffin out of the car and now take off the lid." Then He does the same as He did to the little boy at Nain and gives the boy back to his mother. What an amazing guy to be around. That is what I call amazing! I must be around this man! What about YOU?

The story can be found in the gospel of Luke Ch 7 starting at verse 11.

1 John Ch 5 v 12 states that:

> *He who has the Son has life, He who does not have the Son does not have life* (already dead).

There are so many walking dead in our cities, towns and villages that need to get life, the real life, the life of God. *For as many as are led by the Spirit of God these are the Sons of God. . . . Heirs of God – Joint heirs with Christ.* (Romans Ch 8 v 14 & 17) If the family has a massive fortune and you are the only heir and you are right with the person that owns it all. One day it will be all yours. This is what the scriptures say in 1 Corinthians Ch 2 v 9:

> *But it is written*: (prophesied earlier in Isaiah Ch 64 v 4)
> *"Eye has not seen or ear heard, nor have entered into the heart of man. The things which God has prepared for those who love Him."*

Sometimes we have difficulty in understanding why God allows some things to happen, even bad things and for us to disgrace ourselves in front of everyone. Yet the Lord knows what He is doing, and just like the account earlier about the man in the tombs, when we thought Jesus was doing a pact with Satan. The Devil does not even get a crumb of the loaf where God is concerned.

God foreknew us, He predestined us, He called us, justified us, also glorified us. We are already glorified. The Lord is saying all this so that we can be formed into the likeness of His Son. Now if we are already in glory there are some things inside us that are not going to glory. These need to be dealt with now. We must allow the Lord to deliver us. We need to understand that it was all paid for at Calvary. We need to under-stand God has given us the authority to do what He has called the Church to do.

If you were on your death bed and you only had a few words to say before you were taken away and all your loved ones were around your bedside. I do not think you would be talking about feeding the cat or weeding the garden etc, but you would speak of that which was most important and close to your heart. 'Think of it'.

> Before Jesus ascended He said these words, Mark Ch 16 v 15:
> *"Preach the Word of God, cast out demons, speak in tongues, and lay hands on the sick".*

This is what He expects of the Church of God. No more, no less.

A man came for prayer. He had had a car accident years ago. It had left his right ankle very weak and it had not grown over the years. His right ankle was about half the size of the left. As we broke the curse and came against the spirit of shock that had entered at the time of the accident, his ankle started to grow and became as healthy as the other one.

JESUS IS WONDERFUL!

A man came to the Church crippled, blind from birth in his right eye, with sugar diabetes, spots all over his body, abused and rejected. Jesus set him free from all these problems, now he can see out of both eyes, he walks and runs, the sugar diabetes has gone and the spots have left him. PRAISE GOD!

One night when we ran an outreach meeting, a lady came to us in a wheelchair after a series of strokes. She had been prayed for many times but this particular night was her night. As we broke a curse on her life, she not only could walk, but she ran around the room. When she arrived home, not only was she healed and delivered from her incapacity but the Lord had also healed her deformed leg from which she had suffered since she was nine years old. Her Pastor then repented before his whole congregation for his unbelief of the miraculous and all his church made a recommitment to Jesus.

PRAISE GOD FOR HER PASTOR!

There is so much liberalism come into the Church that the unbelievers think that anyone who tries to follow this commission is not the Church. They have been brought up to believe by professing Christians, that the Church today is about garden parties, rummage sales, slimming classes, organ recitals, brass band concerts, spring, autumn and winter fairs and harvest and flower festivals. All these can be very nice and very many are pleasant to go to, I do not wish to discriminate the people who do all the good work, and for their help to the church, but the spiritual life is far more important and people must understand that <u>no good work</u> can get us a place in heaven. Then on the darker side some churches promote even yoga, tai-chi, aromatherapy and martial arts (demonic) lessons in their church buildings.

It is amazing that a good percentage of the people today, when being challenged about God and coming to Church believe it is all about dying. Why go to Church they say, I am not ready to die yet? Could this be is the only thing <u>they</u> see the Church represents. Jesus said, "*let the dead bury their own dead*." Maybe it is about time we started to pray for the dead to come alive and show the people that our faith is about life not death.

Satan has so deceived the apparent church and is still doing so, that they are in danger of going the way of the world rather than seek God. Jesus came for one reason only, to seek and to save that which was lost, and to give life in abundance. No wonder judgment is starting at the house of God.

Jesus tipped up the tables when they were doing similar things in the temple. They were selling cattle, goats, doves etc. They thought it was a good thing. They were in the temple courts selling the animals so the people could use them for sacrifice, which was the law at that time. Jesus saw their hearts and took out a whip and tipped up the tables of the money-changers. He said "*My house shall be called a house of prayer.*"

2 Corinthians Ch 11 v 13 – 15:

> *For such are false apostles, deceitful workers, transforming themselves into apostles of Christ? And no wonder! For Satan himself transforms himself into an angel of light. Therefore it is no great thing if his ministers also transform themselves into ministers of righteousness, whose end will be according to their works".*

Jesus created everything, He is the image of the invisible God, He created all the powers, He created the angels, archangels, cherubim and seraphim. As a high ranking angel Satan was once in Heaven, until he rebelled against God and all those angels who rebelled with him were thrown out of Heaven. So they certainly know the Son of God. Once when Jesus was casting out an evil spirit the demon spoke and said, "We know who you are". Jesus commanded the demon to be quiet. They know who Jesus is and they know if you know who Jesus is.

Acts Ch 19 v 13 – 16 states:

> *Then some of the itinerant Jewish exorcists took it upon themselves to call the name of the Lord Jesus over those who had evil spirits, saying, "We exorcise you by the Jesus who Paul preaches." Also there were seven sons of Sceva, a Jewish chief priest, who did so. And the evil spirit answered and said "Jesus I know, and Paul I know; but who are you?"*

The epistle to the Ephesians explains the position that God has given the Church of Jesus Christ. God raised Jesus far above all principality and power and might and dominion and every name that can be named, not only in this age but also in the age which is to come. We, as the Church, have been given this position, not in our own strength, but in the finished work of the cross, when God raised Him from the dead and seated Him at the right hand of God in the Heavenly places. The Lord wants us to know His exceeding greatness of His power to us who believe.

The Devil has power, let us face it; otherwise the whole world would be saved. If the people knew what Hell was really about, they would not choose that way surely? The Devil may have power but he has no authority over a Christian or a Church, except that which he has been given right. Jesus has got all power and all authority and He has placed it in the hands of the Church to work with Him. He is now in Heaven interceding for all the saints, praying that we will rise up and take the battle to the enemy. Well, all it takes is for the Church to get to know the authority that Christ has invested in it and pick up the gauntlet and say 'yes' to Jesus. He will help us to fulfil the tasks that He has chosen His Church to do.

9. TAKING COVER

Ezekiel Ch 28 v 11 – 17 states:

Moreover the word of the Lord came to me, saying "Son of man, take up a lamentation for the king of Tyre, and say to him, thus says the Lord God: You were the seal of perfection, Full of wisdom and perfect in beauty. You were in Eden, the garden of God; every precious stone was your COVERING: The sardius, topaz, and diamond, beryl, onyx and jasper, sapphire, turquoise and emerald with gold. The workmanship of your timbrels and pipes was prepared for you on the day you were created. You were the anointed cherub who COVERS; I established you; You were on the holy mountain of God; You walked back and forth in the midst of fiery stones. You were perfect in your ways from the day you were created, till iniquity was found in you. By the abundance of your trading you became filled with violence within, and you sinned; therefore I cast you as a profane thing out of the mountain of God; and I destroyed you, O COVERING cherub, from the midst of the fiery stones. Your heart was lifted up because of your beauty, you corrupted your wisdom for the sake of your splendour; I cast you to the ground, I laid you before kings that they might gaze at you. "You defiled your sanctuaries By the multitude of your iniquities, By the iniquity of your trading; Therefore I brought fire from your midst; It devoured you, And I turned you to ashes upon the earth In the sight of all who saw you. All who knew you among the peoples are astonished at you; You have become a horror, And shall be no more forever."

The King of Tyre was a real person who obviously was not in the Garden of Eden, but the Lord is referring to the spirit that was in him, namely the Devil. The King was Satan's agent at that time. Our interest in this scripture is about the one who was in the Garden of Eden, Satan in the body of the serpent. When God made him, he was the seal of perfection, a most beautiful covering angel, perfect in beauty and full of wisdom. If he was full of wisdom then, he will be the same today. So why do many assume that he is some sort of delinquent or moron? It seems at one time he was under God's cover. The scripture tells us every precious stone was his covering also he was in charge of covering

> *"You were the anointed cherub who covers".* And *"I destroyed you, O covering cherub".*

He was covering what? It seems as though he was covering the Glory of God. Similar to how the cherubim spread out their wings above the mercy seat in the tabernacle of Moses. Now Satan is in rebellion to God. He was cast out of the Mountain of God. He was an expert in covering. He would know why there had to be covering.

Now he is an expert in getting people out of cover.

He is the enemy of everything good and pure, everything that God desires.

Ezekiel Ch 26 v 13 states:

> *"I will put an end to the sound of your songs, and the sound of your harps" said the Lord.*

I believe that Christians should take extra special care with the worship in the Church, that the praise and worship is going to Jesus and not to glorify the world system as well. In the modern Church, many songs that have been written do not seem like worship. You can go to some church services these days and not hear the Saviour's name mentioned. I was asked to minister in a church in London. Sunday morning was free, after deciding to take a walk in town, I noticed a church meeting just beginning so I went in. There was a large congregation mainly under twenty-five years old, but sadly and for three hours, neither in worship nor preaching, the name of Jesus was ever mentioned. There was however much reference to giving and tithing and church growth, but again no reference to Jesus. We need to be very careful with praise and worship as we have just read Satan was in charge of the worship in Heaven. His desire is to get the worship directed to him rather than to Jesus. On the mount of temptation he even wanted Jesus to bow down and worship him.

Matthew Ch 4 v 8-10 states:

> *Again the Devil took Him up on an exceedingly high mountain, and showed Him all the kingdoms of the world and their glory. And he said to Him, "All these kingdoms I will give You if you will fall down and worship me." Then Jesus said to him, "Away with you Satan! For it is written, You shall worship the Lord your God, and Him only you shall serve".*

The Lord desires that His children be blessed. The Devil desires that they be cursed. Satan even tried to deceive the Lord. So how can we have even half a chance of getting topside of the evil one unless we take seriously the Word of God? When the word 'covering' is used in Christian circles, people are usually referring to some higher authority like Bishops and Archbishops but this can turn out to be a travesty if those in authority are unbelievers in the Word of God. I believe the subject of covering has a far greater meaning. I totally agree with teachers of the Bible like the late Derek Prince and the late Watchman Nee on the subject of covering. First of all let us deal with God's creation order.

In the beginning God had a plan – Genesis Ch 1 v 26 – 28 states:

> *Then God said "Let Us make man in Our image, according to Our likeness; let them have dominion over the fish of the sea, over the birds of the air, and over the cattle, and over all the earth and over every creeping thing that creeps on the earth." So God created man in His own image; in the image of God He created him; male and female He created them. Then God blessed them, and God said to them, "Be fruitful and multiply; fill the earth and subdue it; have dominion over the fish of the sea, over the birds of the air, and over every living thing that moves on the earth".*

So God created man. The book of Genesis also tells us at the time God made Man (Adam), there was no woman around. This is most important Adam was the name given to Mankind. The woman was still in the man, in the form of a rib when God made him. Adam could not find a companion for himself. The Lord took out a rib from Adam and made woman. So in the relationship of man and woman, when a couple get married, on that day all that is happening is that the rib is coming back to its rightful place, back by man's side. That is why God hates adultery and fornication, because man has too many ribs and no commitment to each other. Also likewise why homosexuality is an abomination to God, and anyone practicing all these abominations will never enter the Kingdom of God. This scripture can be found in 1 Corinthians Ch 6 v 9. If we read on in Genesis, we find that the serpent deceived the woman and she sinned first. A serpent is a living thing that moves on the earth, exactly what the Lord God told our great ancestors to have dominion over.

One would have thought that because God is all-powerful (omnipotent) and all-seeing (omniscience) that He could have intervened in the situation and stopped the woman taking the forbidden fruit. The thing is, God could not and if He could, He would not, because God established in His word that man made in God's image and likeness with a body of dust, would be the one to have dominion on the Earth and God will never go back on His word. Mankind is the only being that has the legal right on this Earth. When God speaks it is established. e.g: Genesis Ch 1 v 3, *Then God said, "Let there be light' and there was light."*

God made a man of dust and breathed into him the breath of life (spirit).

Before God made man, Satan was thrown out of Heaven, a spirit with nowhere to go. The Lord said in that passage in Ezekiel that the Devil would be no more forever. God made Adam (mankind) to have dominion on the earth. That is why Satan needed to get into the serpent so he could take the dominion away from mankind. Afterwards God cursed the serpent and told him that he would have to crawl on his belly forever. The serpent had not always been cursed because when God created everything He said it was *"very good"*, so that must have meant the serpent also. The serpent loaned his body to Satan, because of this, God cursed the serpent. Satan and his agents need to live in a body otherwise he knows he cannot fulfil his plans. Satan and his demons are illegal immigrants. Spirit beings need to live in a body to operate on the earth. They can only get authority when man gives it to them. So whoever or whatever becomes invaded, becomes cursed. Praise God for Jesus as he came to set the captives free. He took the curse on the tree.

Now as mankind had lost dominion on the Earth, God could not intervene; otherwise He would have gone back on His word and He could never be trusted again. God had to find a suitable body to live in so He could come to Earth, that we could be restored back to our legal position that God gave to Adam in the first place. He came in the likeness of man at the appointed time, conceived in the womb of a young Jewish virgin, but first – even she had to be willing. The account can be found in Luke Ch 1 v 26 - 38

> *Now in the sixth month the angel Gabriel was sent by God to a city of Galilee named Nazareth, to a virgin betrothed to a man whose name was Joseph, of the house of David. The virgin's name was Mary. And having come in, the angel said to her, "Rejoice, highly favoured one, the Lord is with you; blessed are you among women!" But when she saw him, she was troubled at His saying, and considered what manner of greeting this was. Then the angel said to her, "Do not be afraid, Mary, for you have found favour with God. And behold, you shall conceive in your womb and bring forth a Son, and shall call His name Jesus. He will be great, and will be called the Son of the Highest; and the Lord God will give Him the throne of His father David. And he will reign over the house of Jacob forever, and of His kingdom there will be no end."*
>
> *Then Mary said to the angel, "How can this be, since I know not a man?" And the angel answered and said to her, "The Holy Spirit will come upon you, and the power of the Highest will overshadow you; therefore, also, that Holy One who is to be born will be called the Son of God. Now indeed, Elizabeth your relative has also conceived a son in her old age; and this is now the sixth month for her who was called barren. For with God nothing will be impossible." Then Mary said, "Behold*

the maidservant of the Lord! Let it be to me according to your word." And the angel departed from her.

Mary was willing for God to work out His plan in her. Just like Satan needs a body to live in, so does God when He is on this Earth. When we pray the prayer Jesus taught His disciples we say:

> Our Father in Heaven,
> Hallowed be thy name.
> Your kingdom come.
> Your will be done
> On Earth as it is in Heaven.

We are saying, "Lord we give you the right to have your way. Here I am Lord! Use me. I make myself available for You to work through me." That is why Jesus had to go through all that He went through.

1) To buy back our freedom

2) So the Holy Spirit could come and reign and live in all who would invite Him to.

We - need to be like Mary who said, *"Let it be to me according to your Word".*

A good prayer would be something like this:

> Lord Jesus, You knew me in my mother's womb, You have predestined me, You have called me and You have chosen me. Here I am, establish Your plans though me, I am willing to give You my body as a living sacrifice, make me wholly acceptable in Your sight. Amen.

Going back to the beginning. It was the woman who transgressed and made an opening for sin to come into the world. Now some say it was the man's fault because Adam should have been in control of his woman. I do not think this is quite the case, they were both given freewill. Is it right for a man to control his wife like some religions do? It is not man's job to control, but to love, and the woman's role to submit to her husband by her own freewill.

Ephesians Ch 5 v 22 – 29 states:

Wives, submit to your own husbands, as to the Lord. For the husband is the head of the wife, as also Christ is the head of the church; and He is the Saviour of the body. Therefore, just as the church is subject to Christ, so let the wives be to their own husbands in everything. Husbands, love your wives, just as Christ also loved the church and gave Himself for her, that He might sanctify and cleanse her with the washing of water by the word, that He might present her to Himself a glorious church, not having spot or wrinkle or any such thing, but that she should be holy and without blemish. So husbands ought to love their own wives as their own bodies; he who loves his wife loves himself. For no one ever hated his own flesh, but nourishes and cherishes it, just as the Lord does the church.

When Adam was created, God said everything was very good. Adam was in total unity with his rib at that time, and I believe this type of unity is what the Lord requires for marriage relationships. The Bible tells us that Woman was first deceived and became a sinner.

1 Timothy Ch 2 v 14.

And Adam was not deceived, but the woman being deceived, fell into transgression.

In my experience, out of every fifty people involved in witchcraft approximately forty nine are women. Out of every fifty occult new age therapists, we have the same statistics. This suggests that there is a weakness in women in the area of deception. Nevertheless it was a woman who had the greatest privilege bestowed upon her that any individual could possibly have from God. It was to carry in her womb and give birth to the Son of God.

If we look at Adam, God instructed him to what he could do and what he could not, we read in Genesis Ch 2 v 16-17:

And the Lord God commanded the man saying, "Of every tree of the garden you may freely eat; but of the tree of the knowledge of good and evil you shall not eat, for in the day that you eat of it you shall surely die."

This was before God made woman. Adam must have instructed woman, for when the serpent tempted her she replied,
Genesis Ch 3 v 2-3:

> *"We may eat the fruit of the trees of the garden; but the fruit of the tree which is in the midst of the garden, God has said, 'You shall not eat it, nor shall you touch it, lest you die.'"*

Notice the woman added to the original words that God instructed Adam maybe she had got a reverent fear of the Lord at that time. Or it could have been that Adam had, and he tried to impress it on the woman.

Psalm 111 v 10 states:

> *The fear of the Lord is the beginning of wisdom.*

Unfortunately she was deceived, Adam knew the truth, yet he rebelled as he did not even question the woman when she gave him the fruit of the tree.

Genesis Ch 3 v 6 states:

> *So when the woman saw that the tree was good for food, that it was pleasant to the eyes, and a tree desirable to make one wise, she took of its fruit and ate. She also gave to her husband with her, and he ate.*

So we see rather than the unity which God commands, everything is chaos and out of order. Things have not changed much since creation even in the Church of Jesus Christ. The Holy Spirit has revealed to the church how things should be; unfortunately mankind has not changed much over the centuries. Now I will endeavour to look at God's order for the Church and family of believers?

1 Corinthians Ch 11 v 1 – 16 states:

> *Imitate me, just as I imitate Christ. Now I praise you, brethren that you remember me in all things and keep the traditions just as I delivered them to you. But I want you to know that the head of every man is Christ, the head of woman is man, and the head of Christ is God. Every man praying or prophesying, having his head covered,*

dishonours his head. But every woman who prays or prophesies with her head uncovered dishonours her head, for it is one and the same as if her head were shaved. For if a woman is not covered, let her also be shorn. But if it is shameful for a woman to be shorn or shaved, let her be covered. For a man indeed ought not to cover his head, since he is the image and glory of God; but the woman is the glory of man. For man is not from woman, but woman from man. Nor was man created for the woman, but the woman for the man. For this reason the woman ought to have a symbol of authority (power King James AV Bible) on her head, because of the angels. Nevertheless, neither is man independent of woman, nor woman independent of man, in the Lord. For as woman came from man, even so man also comes from woman; but all things are from God. Judge among yourselves. Is it proper for a woman to pray to God with her head uncovered? Does not even nature itself teach you that if a man has long hair, it is a dishonour to him? But if a woman has long hair, it is a glory to her; for her hair is given to her for a covering. But if anyone seems to be contentious, we have no such custom, nor do the churches of God.

The Lord gives the order but mankind is changing the order to suit themselves. I believe that God's full blessing can only come to the Church when they get God's creation order right. It is amazing that so many people get upset with this teaching. Sometimes the man gets upset because he is under the woman's control and if he makes a stand, there is war at home. Or the woman gets upset because, she will not give a sign of submitting to her husband because she does not respect him. Maybe he has not given her reason to in the past, or she is part of the free thinking feminist movement. This, in the light of this scripture, is rebellion to God's Word, which the scripture states; is as the sin of witchcraft (1 Samuel Ch 15 v 23). If a woman prays or prophesies without covering her head she dishonours her head, her man. This will indirectly cause her man to be in a wrong relationship with God, as part of the man is not right (his rib). If a man prays or prophesies with his head covered (religions do today) they are dishonouring

God. What about the Overseers of Denominations? Men wearing head covering namely Mitres, are they dishonouring God? This is something that needs careful consideration and prayer. Where does that leave the people who submit themselves to the covering of these leaders? Think about it. Particularly when you hear of same sex couples getting married in churches, clergy involved in homosexuality and witchcraft (Druids, Freemasonry). Some do not accept the Creation or the Virgin Birth or the Resurrection or Eternal Damnation for unbelievers. Some think that there is a place called Purgatory where they can be either prayed out or paid out.

Psalm 49 v7-9 states:

> *None of them can by any means redeem his brother, nor give to God a ransom for him-For the redemption of their souls is costly, and it shall cease forever - That he should continue to live eternally, and not see the Pit.*

No Pope, Bishop or Clergy or any other religion, only the Lord Jesus Christ can save. We might here of other faiths becoming Christians but rather than obeying God and accepting the scripture about covering for women or not covering for men. Many men try to compromise by still wearing a small skull cap or turban especially when in the presence of others. In the epistle to the Galatians Ch 2 v 11-13 we read where the apostle Peter played the hypocrite as well, but the apostle Paul rebuked him.

> *Now when Peter had come to Antioch, I withstood him to his face, because he was to be blamed; for before certain men came from James, he would eat with the Gentiles; but when they came, he withdrew and separated himself, fearing those of were of the circumcision. And the rest of the Jews also played the hypocrite with him, so that even Barnabas was carried away with their hypocrisy.*

In this scripture we see where Paul had to rebuke Peter for his hypocrisy as Peter was agreeing with those who were of the "circumcision," those who were trusting in the law. If that is so then why do some say today that the principal of head covering is going back to the law or going into legalism? If that is true then Paul was a hypocrite, because he would be doing the same as Peter was with the men in Antioch. In fact Paul goes on to say in Galatians Ch 2 v 21:

I do not set aside the grace of God; for if righteousness comes through the law, then Christ died in vain.

Paul also said in the book of Philippians that he used to be a Pharisee and in the righteousness which is in the law, he was blameless. Yet he goes on to say he counted it rubbish that he may gain Christ. It is the same Paul who was so adamant on the scripture on head covering in the First epistle to the Corinthians that he says, we (meaning all the Apostles) have no other custom (practice/way of behaving) neither do the churches of God. Now we must understand the churches of God included Jewish and Gentile churches.

Going right back in Genesis in the account of Isaac and Rebekah; Abraham sent his servant to find a wife for his son Isaac, when he had found the one the Lord had chosen she went back with the servant to meet Isaac.

Genesis Ch 24 v 63 – 65:

And Isaac went out to meditate in the field in the evening; and he lifted his eyes and looked, and there, the camels were coming. Then Rebekah lifted her eyes, and when she saw Isaac she dismounted from her camel; for she had said to the servant, "Who is this man walking in the field to meet us?" And the servant said "It is my master." <u>So she took a veil and covered herself</u>.

This was before the Law was given. They were not under Law at that time, yet this divine principal was obeyed by the chosen woman of God. It was the same for the early church, after all Jesus is the same Yesterday, Today and Forever.

Some today would say it was only the custom of that time we are now in the twenty-first century we do not need this teaching it is not popular. The original apostles' teachings are for the church of Jesus Christ and preachers and evangelists today should be more concerned with being popular with God than being popular with man. Dear reader we might be in the twenty-first century but the Word of God is the same. Sin is the same and the Devil is the same. Some say the Bible is old fashioned and we have moved on throughout the centuries, well, if we have moved on, sin is old fashioned, so why do people still do it? As we are in the twenty-first century we must be all the nearer to Christ's returning, so should we not be exceptionally vigilant. Some say the Corinthian women who were harlots never covered their heads, so the apostle Paul told the ladies to do so when praying and prophesying in the church. If this was so why did he not tell them to do so whilst walking the streets of Corinth? Well, there are harlots around today. There are some maybe, who may call themselves Christians?

Some would say it does not really matter it is only a symbol; it is what is in your heart that counts. These people are right; of course, we must have a heart for God and His Word. We have already dealt with the subject of symbols so I do not feel the need to recap. It is very important what is in your heart, and if your heart is for God's Word, why not obey Him? Some people disagree and say that the woman's hair is her covering because of the part of the scripture i.e. verse 15 that says that *"her hair is given to her as a covering"*. If that is so, why did the apostle say only six verses earlier *"let her be shorn"*? Verse 15 means her natural covering. God in His graciousness gave woman hair for her beauty (scripture describes the woman's hair as 'her glory' and also she is the glory of man and man is the image and glory of God). He could have made 'Eve' bald. I ask you 'Has Satan so deceived the Church that we are blind to this scripture? Could it be that the Devil, as he understands about covering and was an expert in the matter, has revealed to some false religions a little bit of truth and allowed them to take this truth too far. Consequently what some religions practice becomes so abhorrent to mankind and God, that the modern church has discarded the whole teaching. The Bible tells us we should have the mind of Christ which we must strive for.

As I write this book, hostages have been taken in Iraq with the hope of holding the French government to ransom, for not allowing the Hijab (Muslim headscarves) to be worn in the schools. Can you see Satan's deceptive methods, to make it even more a controversial subject to the body of Christ as we are approaching these last days? Even though the Word of God states that only in prayer and prophesying does He require a woman to cover her head? Satan has defiled this divine principal and it seems that

maybe the Church has been hoodwinked.

Christ has set us free, yet we as Christians must not assume that our freedom in God means that anything goes, otherwise we could be in danger of ignoring this vital scripture to our peril? The scripture in Verse 10 is an interesting verse. "Authority on her head because of the Angels". The King James AV states "Power on her head." Does a woman need power or authority over the good angels that love her and are on her side, or the fallen angels who hate her and want to kill and destroy her? This teaching is not because Paul was a woman hater as some try to say.

2 Timothy Ch 3 v16.

> *All scripture is given by inspiration of God, and is profitable for doctrine, for reproof, for correction, for instruction in righteousness, that the man of God may be complete, thoroughly equipped for every good work.*

All the scriptures were written by the inspiration of the Holy Spirit and He loves us. Satan is the instigator of sickness and disease hence the scriptures are given for our protection. I heard a man I greatly respected speaking to a congregation of about two thousand men and women. The subject was "Being a Servant" and finally, he addressed the ladies saying, "Ladies you should cover your heads when you pray, but if you have more of the fear of man than you have the love of God then you will not do it."

Proverbs Ch 29 v25 states:

The fear of man brings a snare

How sad it is if Christians have been caught in a snare, because of their fear of one another. Should not we have a reverent fear of God?

Isaiah Ch 4 v 1 – 6 states:

> *And in that day seven women shall take hold of one man, saying, "We will eat our own food and wear our own*

apparel; only let us be called by your name, to take away our reproach." In that day the Branch of the Lord shall be beautiful and glorious; and the fruit of the earth shall be excellent and appealing for those of Israel who have escaped. And it shall come to pass that he who is left in Zion and remains in Jerusalem will be called holy- everyone who is recorded among the living in Jerusalem. When the Lord has washed away the filth of the daughters of Zion, and purged the blood of Jerusalem from her midst, by the spirit of judgment and the spirit of burning, then the Lord will create above every dwelling place of Mount Zion, and above her assemblies, a cloud and smoke by day and the shining of a flaming fire by night. For over all the glory shall be a covering. And there will be a tabernacle for shade in the daytime from the heat, for a refuge, and for a shelter from the storm and rain.

In the first part, the scripture explains the case for the woman who is not married in the Church, they will look after themselves either single or widows, but will lay hold of one man (they come under the Leadership of the Church.) It also says the fruit of the earth will be excellent, (man was made of the earth, healed and restored.) For over all the glory there will be a covering. King James AV. states: "*For over all the glory there shall be a defence*". The woman's hair is her glory. A covering or defence is needed for the woman.

The scripture tells us why she needs this defence. From the daytime heat, a refuge (a place of safety) and a shelter (a hiding place). Somewhere to shelter from the storm and the rain as in Ch 5. of this book. Baal the husband of the sexual goddess Ashtoreth is the god of storm and rain. A refuge and a shelter from the works of the Devil, the demon powers. Again we see a symbol as a powerful thing. If at least half of the Church congregation is seemingly deceived into rebellion (i.e. if this scripture in 1 Corinthians Ch 11 is still part of the Word of God), also we must remember the stern warning from the apostle Paul when he said "*we have no other custom, nor do the churches of God*". It could leave a devastating problem for the Church of God, if it is ignored. Some would say that there are some great women preachers who do not cover their heads, which is true, because God's gifts and callings are irrevocable. Praise God for all of them. We must never forget the slave girl in Acts Ch 16 she was preaching the truth as well. This principle is not about whether a person is saved or not. That is determined at the cross of the Lord Jesus Christ. It is not a matter of receiving more blessings that the Lord has for us. The gifts of God are from the Holy Spirit and are for both men and women. It is a matter of respect and reverence towards God and accepting His governmental order. In creation order

Man is Man and Woman is Woman.

When the woman covers her head in prayer it is a sign to the good angels that she accepts the Lord's governmental protocol, and to the fallen angels under Satan's control it is sign that she is not being rebellious like Eve. Satan cannot read our hearts but he can see what we do and how we react and he does understand symbols. His demons are waiting for a chance to strike. We must not give him a foothold. Surely in the light of this revelation Christians must carefully consider this teaching on covering especially in prayers of intercession and spiritual warfare. We surely want our prayers to be heard on High. Can we always be sure that it is the Lord who answers? If we have sin in our lives the Bible tells us God will not hear from on High, even with fasting.

Isaiah Ch 58 v 4 states this:

> *Indeed you fast for strife and debate, and to strike with the fist of wickedness. You will not fast as you do today to make your voice heard on high.*

When we pray, our prayers are taken by the angels to the throne of God. The angels are ministering spirits, the book of Hebrews Ch 1 v 14 states:

> *Are they not all ministering spirits sent forth to minister for those who will inherit salvation?*

One of their jobs is to try to take the prayers up to God, by first passing through the lower heavens in which the Devil and his demons are very active. In the light of the scripture in Corinthians which I have already explained *"authority or power on the woman's head"*. The demonic realm very likely could abort the prayers of the saints. The good angels have to confront the Devil and his angels, before getting to God's throne. Think about It!

The book of Jude v 9 states:

> *Yet Michael the archangel, in contending with the Devil, when he disputed about the body of Moses, dared not bring against him a reviling accusation, but said, "The Lord rebuke you".*

There was a dispute between Michael and Satan, two of the prominent angels both originally in Heaven, one obedient and one disobedient. Both knew God's righteousness and His ways. Michael had to put the matter into the Lord's hands. Maybe it was because Moses was not allowed into the Promised Land because he acted out of anger when he struck the rock in the wilderness rather than speaking to the rock as God commanded. The account can be found in Numbers Ch 20 v 7-12. <u>A little thing we might say, but Satan noticed and took note</u>. All I can say is

PRAISE GOD FOR JESUS.

Matthew Ch 18 v 20:

> *For where two or three are gathered together in my name, I am there in the midst of them.*

The Lord is just waiting to work, but as He gave the dominion of this earth to man, we have to invite Him to intervene. Here is a true account that happened to me.

After being saved and set free, I still attended a denominational church, where we had a new minister. After a few months someone told me that the church had Yoga classes in the evenings. I approached the minister and he was quite happy because they paid for the hire of the room, and the money was good for the church. I said what I thought, that Yoga was from Hinduism so how can we even allow it, however much they pay. I told him that I was not happy with his response, so he said he would ask the area superintendent. He agreed with the minister, I said that I was not happy with that either, so he said that he would take it to national level. In the end I realized that I was getting nowhere.

My wife, a friend and I, spoke about the situation, and we were all in agreement. Then we prayed. Nothing special just, "Lord close down the Yoga meetings in Jesus name. Amen"

The Yoga meetings closed down almost immediately. THANK YOU JESUS!

In our local town there was an occult shop. Some of the churches were praying against this for a few years. As I was walking through the town one day the Lord told me to go in. Not knowing what to expect I went in and proceeded to look at the titles of the books on the shelves. The man asked me if I needed any help. I said "I cannot see any books on these shelves that glorify God, why is that?" After receiving some abusive language. The Holy Spirit came upon me and I replied, "I give you notice that in six months time as from this day this shop will be closed," then I walked out.

The shop closed as I had prophesied.

We have encountered similar instances with other businesses that have tried to stop the preaching of the gospel. The Lord has done the same. PRAISE GOD!

The Lord is saying if only two or three are gathered He is there. A husband and wife team can be very powerful if they are right with God. Men, we need to love and protect our ladies and not be unaware of the Devil's cunning schemes. He might be full of wisdom and he might whisper in people's ears that it does not matter, but he is a liar and father of lies.

Surely people of God, the Lord knows best. Surely He is on our side? If you cannot believe that, how can we ever hope to be saved from the Devil's grip? The Church of Jesus Christ has all the power and authority to take the battle to the enemy. I believe for too long the Church has just been struggling to exist and having to put up with the Devil's works, yet the Church just continues to grin and bare it. For too long the Church has been reactive rather than proactive. The old Hymn by Arthur Sullivan starts with the words in the first verse.

Onward Christian Soldiers marching as to war.
Looking unto Jesus who has gone before.
Christ, the Royal master, leads against the foe.

He is our commander in chief.

It also has a verse that starts with the words

Like a mighty army
Moves the Church of God.

And finishes with the words

We are not divided,
All one body we-
One in hope and doctrine,
One in charity.

The Bible tells us that the Lord wants to pour out His blessing on the Church. Unity is the key. Many scriptures talk about unity, but surely; not unity at any cost. Not the cost of denying His Word. A friend of mine whom I respect greatly as a Christian Minister once said, 'A ton of unrepentant prayer will not make up for an ounce of disobedience'. You know that is quite true. The Lord wants us to accept His Word like a little child, not to be childish but to receive His Word with joy, trusting that what He says is the best for us.

Everything in the Bible is written by the inspiration of the Holy Spirit so why do people when they do not agree say something like, 'Oh it was Paul's word, his idea or Peter's idea not Gods'. Now you know that is not true. I know if the Bible says something and I do not or will not agree I know full well I am wrong. The Church can be glorious and victorious, God wants it to be and so do all of the Christians I believe. Satan wants to steal, kill and destroy. We truly need to allow the Lord to have His way in the Church and in our lives. He wants to rule, He wishes to bless and set free. He wants to use His children to show the world that Jesus truly is alive and reigning in the Church, King of Kings and Lord of Lords, Victorious Mighty God, Everlasting Father, Wonderful Saviour, Master Healer and Deliverer. Jesus Christ the same Yesterday, Today and Forever.

Surely goodness and mercy shall follow me all the days of my life; and I will dwell in the house of the Lord forever. Psalm 23 v 6.